Rosemary Gill devised and wrote the BLUE PETER BOOK

90p

And pride of place on the cover of our Twelfth BLUE PETER BOOK goes to a very special pin-up – Petra.

We think Petra must be just about the most popular dog ever to have appeared on television, and that's why we've given her two whole pages of our new book all to herself. And while Petra's been seen more on television screens than most people have had hot dinners, we've news of another dog who made her very first public appearance less than one year ago. You can read all about Buttons, our new Blue Peter Guide Dog puppy, on page 26, and about the many other things your 3 B's have helped to provide for blind people all over Britain.

Talking of our Appeals reminds us of a piece of marvellous news about our 1974 Stampede in aid of the victims of the terrible drought and famine in Ethiopia. Because of the extremely disturbed political situation, it was impossible to get news from Addis Ababa about our two big projects – the irrigation scheme in the Danakil Desert, and the oxen we gave to the people of Dinser. But last January our on-the-spot reporter, Tony Hall, flew to Britain and came to our studio to give us up-to-date eye-witness accounts of how both schemes were progressing. The news was better than we'd ever dared to hope. Out of our 400 oxen, only three had died, and in spite of the fact there had been very little rain, the people of Dinser had managed to produce a harvest of teff. Hundreds of miles away, the nomadic Afar tribe had also had a harvest – of cotton. And this was entirely due to the success of the irrigation scheme, which Tony told us had transformed the previously barren area into a small oasis.

Back in Britain, we've been having our own Blue Peter harvest. Thanks to Percy Thrower, our garden has produced a whole range of delicious vegetables, astonishing when you think it's only a small patch 3½ metres by 3½ metres. Percy got us off to a good start as you can see on page 68, but don't forget it's the weeding and the watering that are half the battle!

Still, anything that saves money is worth a bit of extra effort. We've enjoyed thinking up things to make that are a fraction of the price you'd have to pay in the shops, and we've included some of the most popular ones in this Twelfth Book. Don't forget, it doesn't matter if you haven't got the exact materials we use. You can always add your own ideas, and often they can result in even better end-products.

Looking back, the last year has been full of narrow escapes – some of them really hairy, too! Like the time we were all trussed up in very uncomfortable harnesses for our famous Flying Ballet. There could have been some serious accidents if we'd collided in mid-air in the roof of the Blue Peter studio.

Peter was almost cut off by the tide when he was up to his thighs in thick, slimy mud during his shrimping expedition, and had a motorbike ridden over him when he trained with the Royal Signals Motorbike Display Team. But perhaps John had the luckiest escape of all. His crash at 80 m.p.h. on his two-man Bob Sleigh Run could have been fatal. As it was, he got away with a great deal of backache and some eye-shattering bruises. It all goes to show there's never a dull moment working on Blue Peter – but perhaps it's just as well we never know what's going to happen next!

Petra   Jason   Shep

P.S. Don't forget page 77.

4

1

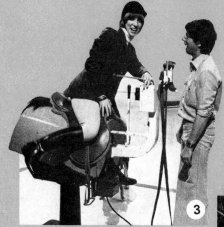

2

3

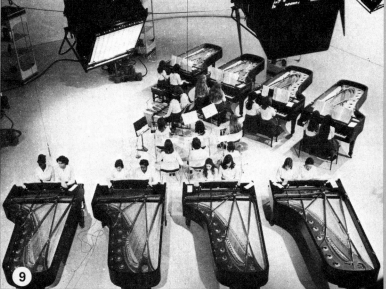

4

5

6

7

8

9

Coronation

I never thought I'd ever take part in a ceremony with five Kings and Queens, and two Princes and Princesses. But that's what happened on 1 November 1974, when I helped at the Coronation of the new King and Queen of Hackney.

It all started with one of Val's very first Blue Peter Special Assignments. When she was filming in London, one of the places she reported on was Petticoat Lane, the world-famous street market. It just so happened there was a Royal Visit taking place at the time in the shape of His Majesty the Pearly King of the City of London.

His Majesty, King George Hitchen, looked resplendent in his magnificent pearly suit – but Val noticed there were one or two gaps where some of the pearl buttons were missing. King George said it was because nowadays they were hard to come by – and that chance remark resulted in a deluge of supplies. We received hundreds of sympathetic letters, and with each one came a parcel of buttons for His Majesty. Altogether Blue Peter viewers sent over 70,000 pearl buttons – enough for King George to make a brand-new suit, and also complete outfits for a new Pearly King and Queen.

Sixteen months later, the new King and Queen were crowned, and we took Blue Peter cameras to film the ceremony in London's East End. The coronation took place in an old people's home in Hackney, but before the actual crowning, there was a sit-down dinner for the Old Folks, and a grand entertainment

Children, dogs, babies – every member of a Pearly family wears the distinctive pearly patterned clothes. The earliest pearly outfits were "smothered". With the buttons sewn together so closely, not a glimpse of material could be seen.

Prince Paul and Princess Janet, whose coronation I attended, were wearing outfits decorated by buttons provided by Blue Peter viewers. So was their grandfather, the Pearly King of London.

The Reverend Austin Williams, Vicar of St Martin-in-the-Fields, performed the coronation ceremony. And I stood in the background holding the newly crowned King and Queen's hats.

with displays of tap dancing and all the traditional well-loved cockney songs.

1975 is the centenary of the Pearly Kings and Queens of London, and their importance as part of Britain's traditional way of life will be marked by a special reception at the House of Lords.

The Pearlies are street traders or costermongers. And costermonger is short for costard-monger or a seller of costards – a large kind of apple.

The story goes that in the 1870s London faced an invasion of French street traders who came to this country to sell *their* apples. These rival traders attracted attention by wearing sequins on the collars and cuffs of their jackets. So not to be outdone, the costermongers embroidered their jackets with hundreds of pearl buttons. This produced an even more dazzling effect than the sequins. As many as 25,163 have been known to be sewn on to one costume alone and often hardly a speck of material can

Henry Croft was the first-ever Pearly King. His tomb is at Finchley's St Pancras Cemetery.

be seen through the shimmering iridescence of the mother of pearl.

I felt quite proud that the new King and Queen were to be wearing suits made from Blue Peter viewers' buttons. Their coronation was organised by King George – and it was a real family occasion, because the new monarchs to be were his own grandson and granddaughter, 17- and 15-year-old Paul and Janet Groves. Prince Paul and Princess Janet seemed quite nervous – although as well as their grandfather – King George – to support them, there was their granny – Queen Sadie – their Uncle Fred, the Pearly King of Westminster, and their two step-brothers, King Victor of Hoxton and King Ron of Dalston.

Paul's suit was a replica of the one worn by the first-ever Pearly King – Henry Croft. And if you visit St Pancras cemetery at Finchley, you can see a monument of a Pearly King on Henry's grave, with the words "The original Pearly King". It was erected by a group of hospitals in gratitude for King Henry's fund-raising, and this is another tradition still carried on today.

The Pearly Kings and Queens collect thousands of pounds for charity. Not only by their appearances in Britain, but on overseas tours, too.

In the old days, London had about fifty pearly families, and titles were handed down from generation to generation. Now there are less than 27. Pearl buttons are scarce – and so's the right cloth for the suits and the tailors skilled enough to cut them. The suits themselves are heavy and uncomfortable. They tend to be unbearably hot in summer and very cold in winter. And – most important of all – the younger generation doesn't seem to be all that interested.

But fortunately, Paul and Janet *are,* and it was a moving moment when the Reverend Austin Williams, Vicar of St Martin-in-the-Fields, placed crowns on their heads. This was where I came in – because I had to hold Janet's everyday hat of ostrich feathers and Paul's pearly cap while the ceremony took place.

Later on, I gave them back again – just like Queen Elizabeth II – King Paul and Queen Janet only wear their crowns on very special occasions. And that was the signal for more music. Our Pearly Coronation ended with a right royal knees up!

The Cumberland Giant

We'll never forget the day we met this three-and-a-half-metre-tall giant. And with a chest measuring 230 cm and biceps of 166 cm we were quite glad he was a load of air and rubberised canvas instead of flesh and blood.

Mighty Mick the Cumberland Giant, and Terrible Ted his sparring partner, were designed and created by artist Jules Baker, and Jules also solved what could have been a giant-sized transport problem by inserting a plug in each colossal left leg. When the plugs are pulled out, Mighty Mick and Terrible Ted deflate in a matter of seconds and fold up small enough to be put in the boot of a car.

But fully blown up, the giants raise hundreds of pounds for good causes. Manpowered by Jules, and Rick Luppi, they give riotous wrestling demonstrations. And with pin falls and half nelsons measuring the length of a double-decker bus, it's no wonder that referee Steve Ormrod equips himself with a crash helmet, hooter and truncheon!

CAN YOU RIDE A BIKE?

That was Corporal Bob Barkess's first question when I arrived at Catterick. You may think that's a pretty stupid question to ask someone who's come to spend the day riding with one of the world's top motor-bike display teams.

My answer was pretty stupid as well. I said:

"Well, I'm not quite sure – but I think I'll be all right!"

The Scramble Course across the Moors was killing. The effort of pushing the bike through thick mud nearly finished me off!

But there were compensations!

The course isn't just for fun. Every Dispatch Rider in the Royal Signals must learn to ride through rough country to get vital messages through.

I had actually ridden a bike once, for a few hours, but didn't really think the leader of the White Helmets would be terribly impressed, so I didn't bother him with the details.

We started by riding round and round a flat field with Bob shouting instructions and telling me when to change gear. I also had to get used to riding the bike standing up, jockey style. When you're riding through rough country, "standing up" gives you the extra balance and control. After an hour's basic training, Bob said I could have a go at the Moor's special scramble course, laid out over wild Yorkshire countryside.

"Do you think I'll come off?" I asked him with some trepidation.

"Oh yes," he said, cheerfully, "but there's so much mud about, you're not likely to hurt yourself too badly."

It seemed to me like going in at the deep end; but I was told that all recruits start off on the scramble course. The idea is to give them confidence in themselves and their machines.

"If you can get through that, you can get through anything," Bob told me.

Only a very few of the men going round the course with me would be chosen for the White Helmets, which is the cream of the Royal Signals' motor cyclists. The rest will be trained as dispatch riders which will

mean getting vital messages across rough country when there is no other means of communication.

They weren't going to meet much rougher country than the "Moors" course. It had been a very wet winter and the mud was beyond belief. But it wasn't just muddy fields, we rode through roaring rivers, up hills so steep that my front wheel reared up like a bucking bronco, and down one-in-three gradients which were just one long skid from top to bottom. I came off more times than I can count — over the top — off the back — broadside on — you name it, I fell off it!

The effort of pushing the bike along with my feet when I was up to the hub caps in mud was beginning to tell. The trouble was that the rest of the recruits were much fitter than I was. Every day they're up at six for gym and a four-mile cross-country run before breakfast. Then they start on the motor bikes!

The second time around I was a lot better. I'd built up confidence and felt able to "give it gun" when it came to the really bad bits. My first reaction had been to slow down as I approached deep mud and water, which was absolutely fatal. I was now able to stand up — open the throttle — and attack every obstacle.

That was the morning. By lunchtime I was caked with mud and completely exhausted, but it wasn't over yet. After lunch and a shower,

I couldn't see a thing except the top of the board, but I could hear the roar of the engine as Bob streaked towards me.

Then it was my turn. Bob said, "Open her up — and keep her opened up!"

I felt a sudden jolt — the hot breath of the exhaust on my face — and he was gone!

Luckily for Ted he was wearing gloves, because I rode straight over his fingers!

I went out to join the White Helmets themselves as they went through some of their death-defying stunts.

I rode out with Bob Barkess, both of us carrying a flaming torch to light the straw arch for the famous "ride through fire".

The paraffin-soaked arch burst into flames and immediately, without a second's pause, Signalman Bob Skee roared up the ramp behind us, disappeared into the chasm of flame and shot out the other side.

"I wonder if you'll give me a hand with the next trick," Bob asked.

"What do I do?"

"Just lie down there and stay quite still," he said, placing a long board on top of me.

"Then what?" I asked, peering over the board.

"Well, I'm going to run over you, actually," he said rather apologetically. "Just wait there while I get my bike."

"Are you serious?" I asked incredulously.

"Oh yes," he said flatly. "Just keep your elbows straight and your head to one side, and you should be all right."

Luckily I wasn't able to see him coming from my position under the board, but I could hear him all right — the rasp as he kick-started, the roar as he revved up the engine, then the low scream as he accelerated towards me, that became a high-pitched whine as he hit the base of the ramp. I felt a sudden jolt — the hot breath of the exhaust on my face, and he was gone.

The next bit was even more frightening. I was going to ride the bike while Ted, one of the Helmets, was under the ramp. It's one thing to risk your own neck against the skill of an expert, but it's something else to risk another guy against *your* skill — especially if you've only learned to ride that morning!

But Bob was very reassuring.

"Get into second gear — stand up. I'll be over there. When you get to where I'm standing, open it up — and keep it opened up."

Ted was looking quite resigned as he lay down under the ramp. Whether it was

I made Number 13 on the pyramid driven by three White Helmets (only the members of the team wear the coveted White Helmets).

confidence in me, or a soldier's acceptance of fate, I'll never know. But I did exactly as Bob had told me, hit the ramp in the middle, took off (that was great!) and landed safely on the other side. I was flushed with success. I went round again for another go – but faster. This time I slightly overcooked it, and nearly slipped off the side of the ramp. Ted told me afterwards that I'd ridden straight over his fingers! Luckily his gloves had saved him, and he wasn't hurt at all.

My ramp was 30 cms off the ground, which I thought was pretty good until Bob asked me to act as a bearer for *his* ramp. Signalman Colin Hunt and I were standing upright holding a pole supporting a ramp that was

nearly two metres high. In front of us were four gleaming metres of the Commanding Officer's new white Triumph Dolomite Sprint!

Again, I couldn't see the run up as I had my back to the ramp, but I had a magnificent view of Bob as he shot like a rocket three metres into the air and landed first on his back wheel and then his front as he turned back with a big grin on his face.

The regimental motto of the Royal Signals is Certa Cito, which is Latin for surely and swiftly.

Signalmen have always said it stands for "Get through or bust" which I thought was a pretty fair description of an average day with the White Helmets!

POSTCARD TABLE MATS

Here's an idea for a quick and easy present – and a cheap one, too. These mats would brighten up any tea table, and you can use them for cups and saucers as well as glasses.

Materials:
Picture postcards or pictures from magazines.
Cardboard – e.g. soap packet card.
Glue.
Top of a jar (pattern).
Sticky-backed transparent plastic or clear varnish.
Sticky-backed velour or felt scraps.
Box to put mats in.
Sticky-backed plastic with a pattern to cover the box.

Method:
1 Find a round lid to use as a pattern. You can choose whatever shape you prefer. Square or oblong mats are just as interesting, provided you can find something to make the pattern with.
2 Select the pictures you wish to make the mats with. You can use picture postcards, pictures from magazines, seed catalogues, or birthday cards.
3 Place the lid on the picture, selecting the piece you prefer.

4 Draw round the pattern. Cut out where drawn.
5 Using the same pattern, cut out two pieces of card which will form the reinforcement. (Choose a thin card as it is easier to cut and doesn't blunt the scissors).
6 Glue the three pieces together like a sandwich, making sure that any writing on the card faces inwards.
7 Using the pattern once again, cut out a piece of transparent sticky-backed plastic, and a piece of sticky-backed velour. The transparent plastic will make it easier to wipe marks off the mat.

8 Fix these to the card sandwich which you have already made.

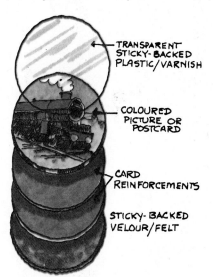

- TRANSPARENT STICKY-BACKED PLASTIC/VARNISH
- COLOURED PICTURE OR POSTCARD
- CARD REINFORCEMENTS
- STICKY-BACKED VELOUR/FELT

9 If you can't get hold of sticky-backed plastic or velour, the mats are just as effective finished off with varnish on the top and add patches of felt underneath.
10 For a final touch you could select a box to cover with sticky-backed plastic, or paint in a bright colour. Then put the mats inside. Remember it's easier to choose the box first and then make the mats.
11 If you have a spare picture, the box will look really nice if you stick a matching picture of your set of mats on the front, e.g. flowers, animals or places.

THAILAND

Do you fancy a dish of ice shavings, topped with sticky green syrup? Or a couple of snakes, perhaps; or a Phra Phrum Spirit House to bring you good luck? Well, we know where you can get them – and that's in any one of Bangkok's amazing floating markets.

A network of waterways surrounds the city. They're called Klongs, and from dawn until the blaze from the midday sun makes it so hot that everyone creeps into the shade, the Klongs become vast boat-jams of floating sampan shops. We visited the Klongs on the first day of our Thailand expedition, and from that moment on, we were knocked out by the bustle and colour of this incredible country.

It's a kingdom; fiercely independent, and one of the few countries in the Far East that's never been conquered by foreigners. In Bangkok, the King has an amazing palace. It's got real gold roofs, so richly decorated with coloured glass flashing in the bright sun that it's almost too blinding to look at. Within the Palace walls, there's a magnificent temple dedicated to the Emerald Buddha. The temple has its own guards, giant statues as high as a house that glare down on the visitors who come from all over the world. To see the temple you have to be correctly and respectfully dressed – and that meant ties and jackets, even though the temperature was up in the hundreds! It was worth it though, to see one of the most famous spectacles in the Orient.

Bangkok is a busy, modern city, with new buildings shooting up every day. Even so, the Thai people haven't lost sight of their ancient traditions. In the heart of the city, there's a remarkable school. It's got a thousand pupils and it's here that both boys and girls come at ten years old to learn the intricate ritual of Thai dancing. About ten or eleven years later, they leave to join dance companies. Each boy or girl is not only able to play the strange Thai musical instruments, and to perform the folk dances, but each one has spent years specialising in performing just one character from the religious story of Rama and his fight for good against evil.

John joined the Monkey God class, and it just about killed him! There was a monkey-like movement to be learnt for everything, from scratching and biting to catching fleas, and each one was more back-breaking than the last.

The girls, too, spend years working on equally complicated movements – balancing on one foot, twisting their fingers to make graceful, flower-like patterns, and just to make it more difficult, they dance with false golden finger nails, 15 cms long, jammed on their finger tips!

Some other neat-fingered people are the sword fighters! Their blades flash like lightning, and fights are rehearsed endlessly, with every move always exactly the same. They have to be, or the swordsmen wouldn't live to fight again! The boxers, too, are almost like dancers, since they fight to music and score points with their feet!

Out in the country life is very different from Bangkok. Most Thai people are farmers, working long hours up to their knees in mud in the rice paddy fields. Whole villages specialise in beautiful craftwork, hand painting paper umbrellas to keep out the sun,

1 Bangkok sparkles! This Temple is roofed with real gold.

2 John goes to dancing class – barefoot on sun-baked concrete.

3 The Third Year teacher makes a monkey out of John.

4 Spiky gold finger nails accentuate the graceful hand movements when these girls dance.

5 Even Lesley couldn't manage the intricate steps.

6 Sparks fly from the blades as these swordsmen go into action. The man in yellow always wins!

7 Threshing rice is hot and heavy work. Every grain has to be bashed off the stalks and collected in the giant bowl.

8 Mid-morning break at the Elephants' School. We fed them sugar cane.

9 Children from the Meo Hill Tribe of Thailand's northern border. They live like cavemen – yet they often go to the cinema.

10 Rice is a non-stop crop. While Lesley was threshing, I was planting seedlings in the muddy paddy field.

11 Imagine making this without a sewing machine! Meo ladies stitch every piece by hand – and weave the cloth, too.

making lacquer bowls and boxes, or carving life-size wooden elephants. Elephants are important in Thailand. There are over 10,000 of them trained to work in the timber industry, dragging the heavy teak logs through jungle impassable to trucks or tractors. There's a special boarding school for them in a jungle clearing in northern Lampang. Not only elephants get taught here, their mahouts go to school with them, too. The elephants start school at five years old, and the boys at fifteen. Five years later they qualify, and

from that first day at school until the elephants are sixty years old, they're never parted. The boy and the elephant spend their whole working lives together and retire on the same day.

Hill tribes inhabit the mountainous country of Thailand's northern border. They've been there for thousands of years, but it's only in the last few that they've come into contact with modern Thailand. A few miles from Chieng Mai, the northern capital, live a tribe called the Meo. They live in frail shelters thatched

7

10

8

11

9

with leaves, growing a few vegetables and hunting jungle animals with their bows and arrows. Only a few years ago, a track was cut through the jungle, just wide enough for a land-rover. Twice a year, gangs of men hack it clear to keep the Meo's new life-line open. They've got a school now, and doctors and nurses come to help them. The young people come into town for a look at the shops, and then a trip to the cinema. They're learning a whole new way to live, and enjoying it, but the old people aren't too sure. It's too soon to say how things will work out for them all. It may be that one day jungle villages like the Meo's will just disappear.

Let's hope, though, that whatever the outcome is, their beautiful craftwork and distinctive black and red dress will survive all the changes.

Talking of things disappearing, one mystery we never did solve was "What happened to the Siamese cats?" Thailand is the country where they were first born and bred. We thought we'd spot Jason's ancestors everywhere, but we never spotted one! Actually, that's not quite true. We did see rows and rows of them – all hand-made in black lacquer and covered with real gold! So even if the Thais are a bit short on the furry kind, they certainly haven't forgotten their Siamese cats!

Bleep and Booster

The devastation and destruction in Miron City was terrible. As Bleep and Booster, green-faced and shaking, picked their way through the twisted girders and smouldering rubble, they could scarcely believe their eyes. Only hours before, a splendid building had housed Miron City's proudest possession – the Total Energiser, the miraculous invention, only the size of a soup tin, that was capable of providing all the energy and power needed to supply the whole of Miron Planet, her cities, industries and space fleets. Suddenly, with no warning, there'd been a scream of engines overhead, and from a vast spaceship had poured hundreds of Devastoids, inhabitants of Devastus, the most feared planet in the galaxy. Though smaller by far than Mirons, the stocky Devastoids, with their beaky noses and scaly limbs, were immensely strong and excessively vicious. Shrieking and yelling, they'd swarmed into the power house, snatched the Total Energiser and utterly destroyed the building. Then, with a last searing blast from their powerful ray guns, the Devastoids had disappeared with their prize, streaking through space in their giant machine.

After the first shock, the Mirons had rallied. Already plans were being made for the Total Energiser's recovery, and Bleep and Booster were on their way to the Space Commando's H.Q. to join a final briefing session. As they slipped into their places, a grave-faced Captain waited to speak.

"Space Commandos," he began. "The situation is critical. The Total Energiser, as you know, is the source of immense power. For us it is used only for peace. In the wrong hands, it can be turned into a weapon of such tremendous power that it could reduce the whole of our planet to dust."

Bleep clutched Booster in horror.

"That's why the Devastoids stole it," he cried. "They mean to destroy us all!"

"Sh!" whispered Booster. "Your father hasn't finished."

The Captain went on.

"The Devastoids wrenched the Total Energiser from its mounting with such force that, without knowing it, they have activated its detonating mechanism. At this moment they are in possession of a live bomb. They don't know it, but it will explode in just a few hours from now."

"Hooray!" shouted Bleep. "They'll blow themselves to smithereens – and their planet Devastus, too!"

"No, my son," said the Captain quietly. "Reports from the border patrol say that the Devastoids' spaceship has not left Miron. Engine failure overtook them. They have landed on our Outlands and are attempting emergency repairs."

There was a stir of excitement in the briefing room.

"When shall we attack, sir?" cried the Commandos. "Let's get to our ships."

"There will be no attack," rasped the Captain. "To blast our way in there is to risk exploding the Total Energiser. We shall all die, both Devastoids and Mirons. There is only one way to recover it, and that is by stealth. Now listen to my plan. . . ."

An hour later, the Captain watched Bleep and Booster climb into their Space Pod, and as they strapped themselves in, he passed two bundles in to them.

"Goodbye," he said. "I did not want to put this dreadful responsibility on to you, but you are the only two on Miron capable of saving our planet. Your size is your strength. Good luck!"

At that moment, all three knew they might never meet again, but Bleep and Booster hid their fears and set off bravely for the Outlands. They knew their chances of success were slight and as they passed over the border patrols, and minutes later saw the bulky, dimly glowing shape of the Devastoids' disabled spaceship below them, they were almost paralysed with terror.

"This is it!" gulped Bleep. "Shall we go on?"

"We must," gasped Booster. "We'll die if we don't and so will everyone else."

At that moment, there was a scuttling sound at their feet.

"Fido," cried Booster. "How did you get on board?" and he scooped up the little green space dog and clutched him tight. Bleep burst out laughing.

"With him on our side, we're a match for anything," he cried.

Somehow the little stowaway dog made them feel better. Silently they landed the Space Pod in the darkness and carefully opened the bundles the captain had given them. They contained their secret weapon.

They looked at the contents. Inside were two suits, each skilfully made to represent Devastoids. To fulfil the Captain's plan, Bleep and Booster were to use the disguises to penetrate the Devastoid defences, recapture the Total Energiser, and sneak away unseen.

"Do you think this plan's going to work?" said Bleep, doubtfully, as he struggled into the scales.

"It's the best plan we've got," snapped Booster. "Help me get my beak on, and we'll soon find out."

Once in the suits, things seemed more hopeful. They were transformed. In place of Bleep and Booster stood two hideous Devastoids — as like as two peas and exactly the same height and size as the stumpy invaders.

"Phase I completed," announced Bleep, "and no one's spotted us yet. It can't be long now before the explosion. Let's get going."

Hurriedly, they whispered rapidly through Phase II of the Captain's plan. Bleep was to go first — if he hadn't returned within 15 minutes, Booster was to follow and make a second attempt. Parting was dreadful. As Booster watched his friend glide out of sight through the darkness, he knew he might never return.

It took Bleep longer than he thought to sneak past the Devastoid patrols. They were everywhere — some swarming round the damaged engine which had been taken from

the spaceship, others supplying them with tools for the repairs. Dozens more were just sitting around, waiting, their beady eyes darting everywhere.

"I'll never get there," whispered Bleep to himself, as he crept from rock to rock, desperately seeking cover. "It's no good," he decided. "I'll have to trust to my disguise."

Boldly, he stood up, and with a deep breath, strode through the lolling Devastoids and made straight for the spaceship. They glanced up at him, but none of them gave him a second look. They were completely fooled! Confidence rushed back to Bleep, and he marched boldly forward, flung open an airlock and walked straight into the spaceship's central chamber. It was deserted, and there, on a central plinth, stood the Total Energiser! Bleep's heart leapt – he was going to succeed!

Suddenly, the airlock door shut behind him. Bleep turned rapidly, and just behind him stood a stocky figure. For a moment, Bleep froze with horror – then relief swept over him.

"Booster!" he cried. "I didn't realise I'd been so long! Here, give me a lift up – I can't quite reach the Energiser." The squat monster crawled to the bottom of the plinth. Bleep climbed on his shoulders, stretched out and grasped the shining metal prize. At that moment, scaly claws gripped him tightly round the legs and brought him crashing to the ground. It wasn't Booster! A real Devastoid held Bleep in a vice-like grip. Panic swept over him. Desperately he struck out, using the only weapon he'd got – the Energiser! It flashed through his mind that it could explode at any second, but his situation was desperate and he had no other choice. He closed his eyes and crashed it down again and again. When he opened them, the Devastoid lay senseless, and the Energiser was still intact! Although there'd been no explosion, the noise of the fight had

been tremendous. Already Bleep could hear slithery footsteps and shouting voices. If he didn't act fast he'd be trapped! Tucking the Total Energiser into his scaly coat, he flung open the airlock door and rushed to meet his attackers.

"The Energiser's been stolen!" he cried. "Quick! Find the thief!" And he rushed into the thronging, swirling mass of Devastoids and lost himself amongst them.

From the rocky ridge overlooking the spaceship, Booster heard the uproar.

"They've caught Bleep," he moaned. "I must rescue him." And grabbing up Fido and pushing him in amongst the scales, he plunged headlong down towards the throng. Soon he found himself shoved along in a crowd of jostling Devastoids. They were squealing and yelling, and completely disorganised. Each one looked exactly the same as the next, scaly and snarling. Booster looked about him in bewilderment. He, too, looked every inch a Devastoid. His disguise was perfect – and so of course, he realised, was Bleep's!

Somewhere amongst all these hideous monsters was his friend! But which one was he? Despair overwhelmed him. Then, just as the position seemed hopeless, he felt Fido stir inside his jacket. His little whistling bark was quite insistent. Scales and beaks didn't fool Fido! He'd know Bleep's scent anywhere, Booster realised with a surge of relief, and judging by the scuffling, he'd already picked Bleep out of the mob! Booster turned to the Devastoid nearest him and risked a cautious whisper.

"Bleep?" he murmured. Instantly a scaly arm went round him and a voice whispered in his ear, "I've got the Energiser and they don't realise it! Follow me and we'll get it back to Miron City before it explodes. We've just got time!"

Bleep and Booster split away from the crowd and ran for the safety of the Space Pod for all they were worth, but luck was against them. Their sudden move had given them away. A spine-chilling yell went up from the Devastoids, and as one, the whole mob came pelting after them.

"It's no good," moaned Bleep, as they flung open the Space Pod door. "There's no time to fire the engines. We'll never get away!"

"Leave this to me," yelled Booster, "and do everything I do!"

He snatched up a heavy spanner and began to smash the Space Pod controls.

"You, too," he cried to Bleep. "Smash the ship," he insisted. "Any minute now we'll all blow up."

"He's gone mad," thought Bleep tearfully as he kicked in the control panel. "Why are we destroying our only means of escape?"

He saw his friend grab something from the wreckage; the next minute Bleep was dragged outside just as the panting horde arrived.

"Bash up the Miron Space Pod," yelled Booster to the monsters. "Flatten it for ever! Grind it to the ground!"

The Devastoids flung themselves on the vehicle in an orgy of destruction, vying with each other to do the most damage. It made Bleep sick to look at them, but they were so intent on their evil work that they never noticed Bleep, Booster and Fido as they crept rapidly away and hid amongst the rocks.

"Now what?" gulped Bleep, as they crouched in a crevice, clutching the precious Total Energiser. "We're stuck with a bomb that can go up any second, and no one knows where we are!"

"Oh yes they do," cried Booster. "That's why I had to bust the Space Pod. I've got this out!" and he held out to Bleep the little homing device that all Miron Space Pods carried in case of emergency.

"Our signal will already have been picked up. I bet you the Commandos will be here any second!" And he was right!

At that instant, the Space Commando fleet roared overhead, blasting the Devastoids and their spaceship to pieces. The experts were already racing towards them, ready to neutralise the Total Energiser.

The Captain's plan had worked, and Miron planet was saved — thanks to Bleep, Booster and their mini-monster skins!

SPECIAL ASSIGNMENT

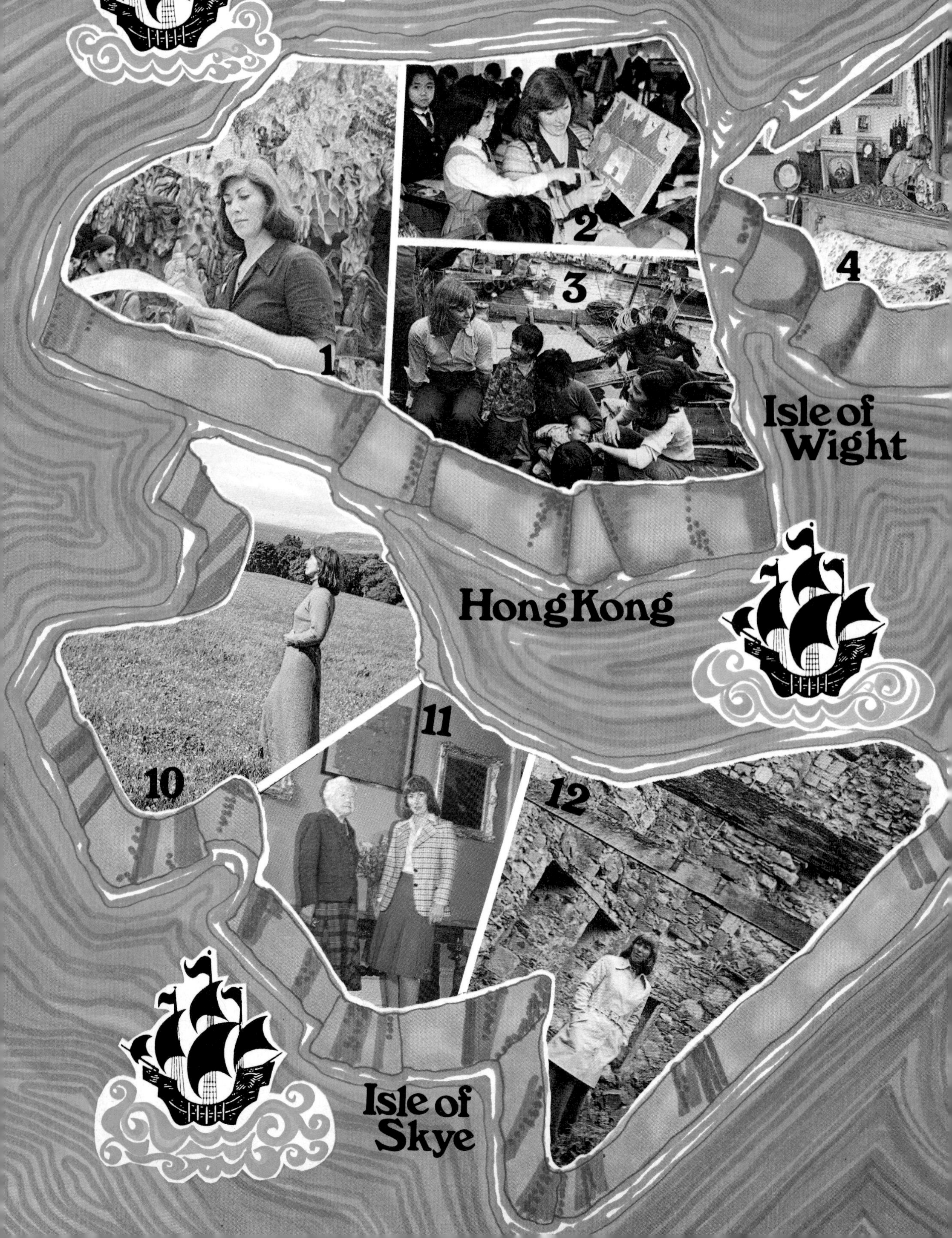

1

2

3

4

Isle of Wight

Hong Kong

10

11

12

Isle of Skye

5

6

9

8

7

5

Isle of
Man

13

14

15

Malta

Do you remember what Val discovered on each of these Islands? (Answers on page 76)

POMELETTE AND PUDDING

You'd never believe that
four eggs could provide a first course
and a pudding for three people – but they can,
if you add a few extras. I've called my first course a
"pomelette" because it's a cross between a pancake and an
omelette, and the lemon surprise pudding really is a surprise,
because people find it hard to guess the ingredients. And with
food becoming more expensive, these two recipes are really economical.

Pomelette

Ingredients

2 egg yolks, 2 whole eggs,
left-over scraps, like bacon,
cold potatoes, ham,
cold vegetables
4 teaspoons of self-raising
flour
1 tablespoon of milk
salt and pepper

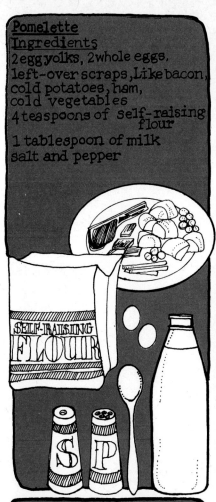

Melt a little fat in a
frying pan, add
left-overs and cook
on a low heat.

While this is cooking,
whisk eggs lightly in a
basin, (saving the
two spare
egg whites)
add
salt and pepper,
flour, milk, and
mix thoroughly.

Pour the egg mixture over
the food in the frying pan
and let it cook.

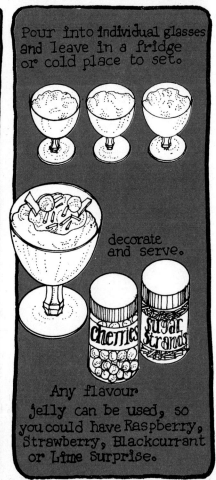

Then turn it over
(piece by piece, don't
try to toss it!)

When properly cooked,
serve on a warm plate.

Lemon Surprise

Ingredients

1 packet of lemon jelly
2 egg whites - 1 left over
from the pomelette.

Make the jelly
with water as
directed on
the packet
and leave
until cold,
but **not**
completely set.

Whisk 2 egg whites
until stiff.

Pour jelly over egg whites

mix gently
until the egg white
is the colour of
the jelly.

Pour into individual glasses
and leave in a fridge
or cold place to set.

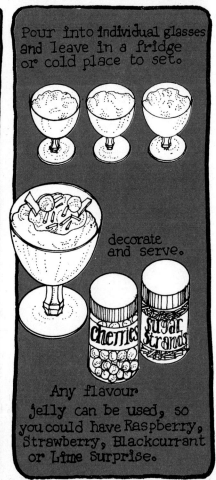

decorate
and serve.

Any flavour
jelly can be used, so
you could have Raspberry,
Strawberry, Blackcurrant
or Lime Surprise.

THE 3B's APPEAL

Eleven years ago, by collecting aluminium foil and silver paper, Blue Peter viewers provided the programme's very first Guide Dog for the Blind. After we had puppy-walked Honey for twelve months, she went to her Training School, and – passing all her tests with flying colours – became the eyes for Miss Elsie Whitehead, a retired school-teacher from Leicester. When we heard that Honey, herself, would soon be due for retirement, we decided it was up to us to supply a replacement. After all, as Blue Peter had provided her in the first place, it was only fair that we should help again. But are Guide Dogs a really good way of helping blind people? Was there something more useful we could provide? And would Miss Whitehead definitely need another dog? I travelled to Leicester to find out.

Our studio Totaliser showed our Appeal Target. We asked for 2,000,000 envelopes of 3 B's.

Down at the Depot the contents of the envelopes were sorted into different categories.

Some of the 3 B's raised money as scrap metal when they were melted down and turned into valuable ingots.

26

By 2 January, we'd reached our target. Derek Freeman brought this litter of seven-week-old yellow labradors to the studio to choose our new Blue Peter Guide Dog puppy.

Thousands of suggestions were sent for the new puppy's name.

"Please come in," said Miss Whitehead as she opened her front door. "Let's go into the living-room. I'm sure you could do with a cup of coffee."

There was nothing I wanted more. It was a freezing cold day in late November, and I'd travelled to Leicester on an unheated train.

Honey was curled up on a blue blanket by the sofa. It was hard to believe that for a dog she was quite an old lady. She looked magnificent – slim and sleek, with a shining coat and a wet nose. She gave me a very warm welcome and settled back on her blanket. Like all Guide Dogs, when their harnesses are taken off, Honey knew she was off duty and could relax.

"Has she really made a difference to your life? I asked.

"It's difficult for a sighted person to understand," said Miss Whitehead. "But to be able to travel freely without always asking other people to help, to be completely independent, is the greatest gift a blind person can be given."

Miss Whitehead went on to explain what life had been like

Honey is Miss Whitehead's third guide dog. She went to school each day while Miss Whitehead was still teaching, and then to evening classes after Miss Whitehead retired.

"I've just passed my O level German exam," she told me. "And I'd never have had the confidence to attempt it, if it hadn't been for Honey."

There was no doubt about it – having a Guide Dog had transformed Miss Whitehead's life. Somehow we had to make sure we provided a successor when Honey retired.

During the next few days we did a lot of research. One of the experts we talked to was an old friend of Blue Peter's, the Guide Dog for the Blind Puppy Walking Manager, Derek Freeman. Derek was very reassuring about what happened to the dogs when they retired. "They don't get thrown on the scrap heap," he said. "All the owners have the chance to keep their dogs as family pets. But if that's not possible, we've a long waiting list of people queueing up to give good homes to our retired Guide Dogs."

That was a great relief. The next thing we wanted to find

Buttons coped well with all the distractions of being out of doors in the centre of London.

Part of Buttons' training was teaching her to climb stairs like this big flight of steps.

It's important to introduce Guide Dog puppies to as many new experiences as possible.

before she'd had a Guide Dog. Every single journey – no matter how short – had meant asking someone to go with her, or else arranging for friends or relations to meet her at tricky points along the route. For instance, as a young girl, Miss Whitehead had gone to college and the journey involved three different bus rides. A sighted person had to be waiting at each bus stop, to guide her on her way.

"Even if your relations are delighted to help, it's dreadful not to be able to do things on your own."

out, was whether or not any mechanical aids had been invented that could give even better help to the blind than dogs. We'd already talked to other guide dog owners, including a physiotherapist and an office worker who told us how lost they'd be without their dogs – but even so, would they be better off with some kind of scientific gadget? Tony Clarke, Director General of the Guide Dogs for the Blind Association, had all the latest news.

"I've just returned from the United States where they've

been experimenting with an electronic system. The idea is that the blind person wears a kind of stomach pad that picks up waves transmitted from any hazards lying ahead. It gives out a warning signal which is fine, except it's all so experimental that there'll be nothing generally available for very many years to come." Tony emphasised how desperate the need for fully qualified dogs was. With a waiting list of hundreds they just can't be trained fast enough. And, of course, with more people using them, more dogs are eventually retiring and having to be replaced, so the demand grows bigger every year.

At the moment there are four Guide Dog Training Centres in Britain – at Forfar in Scotland, at Bolton, Leamington Spa, and Exeter, and there is a Breeding and Puppy Walking Centre at Tolgate – and plans afoot for a fifth Training Centre at Wokingham.

"We've got the planning permission to build the new Training Centre," said Tony. "It's perfect – there are 17 acres of land that are just right for exercising and training the dogs, but there's a lot to do before it's ready. For one thing, we'll need to be able to build a large new block of kennels."

Those words gave us our second idea. As well as replacing Honey, it would be marvellous if we could provide that block of kennels. In that way, we'd be helping to train many more of those extra badly needed Guide Dogs.

So that's how our 3 B's Appeal began. And we decided we'd try and provide the new puppy and the kennels by asking Blue Peter viewers to collect buttons, badges and buckles. With a bit of luck, we'd have some extra valuable donations for a 3 B's Auction, and all the other buttons, badges and buckles could either be offered to dealers, or sold as scrap metal. We decided to aim for a target of two million envelopes of 3 B's (that could be posted for the minimum rate), and in addition, BRS Parcels Ltd made a very generous offer of a nationwide free delivery of parcels.

Our Depot was a huge, disused warehouse by the River Thames – and by the end of the first week of our Appeal, it was already stacked shoulder high with mail-bags full of envelopes, packets, parcels and boxes of every size and shape.

Experts supervised the sorting to make sure all the valuable 3 B's were set aside, and by 2 January 1975 we were able to announce we'd reached our target of 2 million envelopes. Immediately we had this good news, work began, bulldozing the site at Wokingham, and Derek Freeman brought a litter of seven-week-old yellow labradors to the studio to choose our new Blue Peter Guide Dog puppy.

It seemed a hard choice – all the pups looked fit and well and lively. But after examining them and giving them tests like firing a pistol – to see how they'd react to noise – Derek lifted up a plump little bitch.

"I think you'll do very well with her," he said. "And you want to give her a name as soon as you can, because that's one of the first things she'll have to learn."

After sorting out all the thousands of Blue Peter viewers' suggestions – a great many of them extremely good and appropriate, too – it was clear there was one name with about ten times as many votes as any of the others – BUTTONS. So Buttons our new puppy became, and we started our twelve months as her puppy-walkers.

This means that Buttons is brought up almost like an ordinary family pet for a year. At the end of this period, if she passes her tests, she'll go to one of the Guide Dog Training Centres. But at first, every single trainee Guide Dog pup starts off with volunteers who adopt them for a year. It's hard to accept that you'll have to give up the puppy you've trained and grown fond of, but it's worth it if it does eventually become the "eyes" for a blind person. So far we've had tremendous success with Honey, and also with Cindy, our second Blue Peter Guide Dog for the Blind. If Buttons does as well, thanks to our 3 B's Appeal, there'll be three Blue Peter Guide Dogs in action!

This was the second half of our Target – building the Blue Peter Kennels at the new Guide Dog Training Centre at Wokingham.

Derek Freeman showed me round the site – a large tumbledown house with spacious grounds.

We gave a hand with the clearing of the site when we bulldozed some of these old outhouses.

P.S. By 3 February we'd received so many extra envelopes of 3 B's, we were able to give help to all the other Guide Dog Training Centres in Britain.
   Your 3 B's are providing:
1. An extension to the Hospital Block to double up as a maternity ward for Brood Bitches at Forfar.
2. An extension to the Hospital Block to double up as a maternity ward for Brood Bitches at Bolton.
3. An Isolation Block to check any off colour dogs are not carrying infectious diseases at Leamington.
4. An Incubator for prematurely born puppies needing intensive care at Tolgate.
5. A completely piped supply of drinking water for all the kennels at Exeter.
P.P.S. At our 3 B's Sale, held at Phillips on 22 April, enough money was raised to buy and train ten more Guide Dogs for the Blind!

Tuesday, 22 April, was the date of our 3 B's Sale. Phillips' auction rooms were crowded out with people anxious to buy the best of the 3 B's. Buttons sat at Lesley's feet while she worked the calculator to add up the sales.

John took over for one section of the lots. The bidding was fast and furious and Peter acted as porter, holding the lots for all to see.

May 1. As a result of the 3 B's Sale we were able to provide ten more puppies for the Guide Dogs for the Blind Association. There were three Yellow Labradors, two Alsatians, two Border Collies and three Golden Retriever/Yellow Labrador crosses.

Story by Michael Bond illustrated by "Hargreaves"
PADDINGTON CLOCKS IN

Paddington gazed at the Browns' television set as if he could hardly believe his eyes.

"My horse came in at ten to one!" he exclaimed. "But it left at half past twelve!"

The rest of the family exchanged anxious glances. "It doesn't mean your horse took twenty minutes to run the race," explained Mrs Brown. "It's all to do with the odds. Ten to one means you get back ten times the amount you put on."

"Which means I've won thirty matches," said Jonathan. "I bet three matches that *Marmalade* would win and he has."

"You should have stuck to it yourself," broke in Judy.

"He usually does," said Jonathan, trying to make light of the whole affair. "Marmalade, I mean ... er ... that is ... "

But their words were falling on deaf ears. Paddington's attention was still riveted to the television screen.

Until the last race the Browns had been enjoying a quiet game of 'Spot the Winner'. Armed with a list of runners from the daily paper, they had been watching the horse racing at Sandown Park, adding a little spice to the proceedings by taking match-sticks from a pile on the table and placing bets on the various events.

Paddington himself had made a very good start to the day, mostly by working on a system of backing horses whose names he fancied. After two winners in succession – *Portobello Road* in the first race and *Plum Cake* in the second – his pile of used matches had grown quite large, and when they looked up the third race and discovered there was a horse called *Marmalade* running he seemed all set to sweep the board with a hat trick.

But just before the start, Desmond O'Donnelly, the famous BBC Racing Commentator, had let fall a piece of inside information about one of the other runners. It was, he'd said, a tip straight from the horse's mouth, and one so hot he was putting his shirt on the result; a fact which caused Paddington to waver at the last moment and change his bet.

In the event Mr O'Donnelly had not only got his facts wrong but he also seemed to have gone back on what he'd said he would do. Far from losing a shirt, he

appeared to be taking particular pride in displaying his own in all its glory as he beamed over the top of his field glasses at those viewers who were lucky enough to possess a colour receiver.

But it was the simple matter of getting the time wrong that upset Paddington most of all. Even he could see that it was still nowhere near twenty minutes to one, let alone ten to. If hard stares could have been transmitted back through the system to the cameras at Sandown Park, then Desmond O'Donnelly would have dropped his microphone and disappeared down the course faster than any of the horses he was at present trying his hardest to describe.

Paddington came to a decision. "I think," he announced, gathering up what was left of his winnings, "I would like to be excused."

"Oh dear," said Mrs Brown as the door closed behind him, "he does seem to be taking it rather badly. I hope it doesn't put him off his lunch."

"It'll take more than a few lost match-sticks to put that bear off his food," said Mrs Bird. "I'll wager the rest of my matches he'll have got over it before the next lot of horses are under starter's orders."

The Browns' housekeeper knew Paddington's eating habits of old, and it was rare indeed for him to miss a meal, so with that comforting thought in mind she turned her attention back to the television screen.

It was lucky for Paddington that she did, for had Mrs Bird not been concentrating on the commentary her sharp ears might well have caught some ominous rummaging noises going on in one of the upstairs cupboards. They were followed by several short bursts of muffled tinkling, and a moment or so later by the

sound of the front door latch clicking shut; but by then the next race was well under way and everyone was much too excited to notice.

Paddington heaved a sigh of relief when he found himself safely outside number thirty-two Windsor Gardens. He was a bear with a strong sense of right and wrong, but he knew from past experience that he couldn't always count on one hundred per cent support in his campaigns for justice, and he had a feeling that if the rest of the family knew where he was going this might be one of those occasions.

Luckily, no sooner had he closed the front door than a taxi came into view. Paddington didn't normally travel by taxi, but there was no time to be lost, so he decided to jump in and worry about paying for the fare out of his bun reserves later.

"I'd like to go to the BBC Television Centre, please," he announced, as the driver held the back door open for him. "I want to get there before the last race if I can."

"Righto, mate!" As he slipped the cab into gear the driver glanced round and caught sight of Paddington's suitcase. "You can pay me out of your winnings if you like," he chuckled.

Paddington looked most surprised at his unexpected piece of good fortune. "Thank you very much!" he exclaimed. "Mind you," he added doubtfully, "I haven't got very many left after the last race."

"I know the feeling," said the driver sympathetically. "It happens to the best of us."

Glad of an audience, he started up a running commentary on the hazards of gambling in general and backing horses in particular. It lasted for most of the journey; in fact he talked so much that Paddington was barely halfway through the marmalade sandwich he'd brought to while away the time when they reached their destination.

Paddington was a well-known figure at the Television Centre. He'd been there a number of times in the past in order to visit the Blue Peter studios, and as it was a

Thursday the Commissionaire on duty assumed it was another such occasion. As soon as he caught sight of the familiar blue duffle-coat in the back of the taxi he gave a cheery nod, lifted the barrier, and waved them on their way.

Paddington raised his hat politely as they drew to a halt outside the glass doors of the entrance hall. "I shan't be very long," he announced. "But I've got to make sure I get the right person first. I want the man in charge of horse racing," he added impressively.

him," he whispered into the man's ear. "It's due to go off in about five minutes!"

As he climbed out of the cab Paddington felt inside his duffle-coat pocket. "These are my winnings," he explained, pressing his paw into the man's hand. "If you look after my suitcase for me while I'm gone you can keep the change as well."

The driver was too busy wiping the marmalade from his ear to notice straightaway what he'd been given, but when he did open his hand he gazed at it in astonishment. "'ere!" he cried. "What's all this?"

But Paddington had already disappeared from view somewhere inside the vast building.

"Anything the matter?" asked one of the commissionaires as he strolled across and caught sight of the look on the driver's face.

"Anything the matter?" repeated the driver bitterly. "I'll say there is. Look!" And he held out some objects in his hand for the other to see. "That's what's the matter . . . I've just been paid in matches . . . *used* ones at that! Wait till I catch 'im!"

He glanced round his cab and as he did so his gaze alighted on the back seat. A strange look suddenly came over his face. "I'll tell you something else," he cried in

Opening his suitcase, he put the remains of the marmalade sandwich carefully away, made some last-minute adjustments to something else, and then leaned forward and peered through the sliding glass panel behind the driver's head. "I've got a surprise for

alarm, as he jumped out. "I reckon we'd best be getting out of 'ere. If you ask me there's not a moment to lose!"

Unaware of the drama going on five floors below, the man In Charge of Racing Programmes (I.C.R.P. for short) looked impatiently at his secretary. "I really can't have people coming in here to see me unannounced like this," he complained.

"Well, it isn't exactly a *person*," said his secretary uneasily. "And he wouldn't take no for an answer. He said it was very urgent and it has to do with today's racing."

"All right," said her boss wearily. "Show him in." He sometimes wished television programmes didn't have such things as viewers. You could please most of them a good deal of the time, but there was no pleasing everybody all the time.

"I.C.R.P. will see you now," said his secretary, as she ushered Paddington into the room.

"Good afternoon, Mr Arpy," said Paddington, holding out his paw as he advanced across the room. "I'm sorry you're icy. You can borrow my duffle-coat if you like. I'm really quite warm."

The man behind the desk gave Paddington a bemused look. "I really don't quite understand," he began.

"You're lucky I've got it with me," continued Paddington. "I nearly lost it just now."

"You nearly lost your duffle-coat?" repeated the man in charge of racing. "Have you complained to the cloakroom?"

Paddington ignored the remark. "Mr O'Donnelly told me to put my shirt on a horse," he explained patiently. "But bears don't wear shirts, so it could have been my duffle-coat instead."

The man's face cleared slightly. "Do you mean to say you're complaining about one of Desmond O'Donnelly's forecasts?" he asked.

"Yes," said Paddington, glad he'd got his point over at last. "I put my match-sticks on an also-ran and it came in last."

"Well, I'm sorry you're not happy," said the man in charge of racing. "All our commentators are very experienced, but they really can't guarantee a winner every time. Mr O'Donnelly himself has been in the field for a number of years."

"Perhaps that's why he made a mistake with the time," broke in Paddington. "I expect his watch has got damp."

"He said it was ten to one," he continued, warming to his subject, "and it was really only just gone half past twelve. But don't worry, I've brought him a present. It's outside in a taxi."

The I.C.R.P. passed a trembling hand across his brow. He had a strange ringing noise in his head. He wasn't sure if it had to do with his visitior or not, but whatever the reason he wished it would go away.

Before he had a chance to say anything more the door burst open and his secretary rushed into the room. "Quick!" she cried. "The emergency bells are going. Somebody's planted a bomb outside and they're evacuating the building. It's ticking away like mad and they've sent for the disposal squad. Whoever left it said it's due to go off in five minutes!"

Paddington followed the others across to the window, and as he peered through the glass he nearly fell over backwards with astonishment.

The circular forecourt, which a few minutes before had been alive with people as they hurried to and fro about their work, was now deserted. The taxi he'd arrived in was now some distance away, and beyond that again crowds of sightseers were being held back by a bevy of commissionaires who were forming a makeshift barrier.

However, it wasn't all this activity that caused Paddington's alarm; it was the sight of an object surrounded by sandbags just outside the front doors. Even from the fifth floor he was able to recognise it immediately.

"That's not a bomb they're disposing of!" he exclaimed hotly. "That's my suitcase!"

If the entire Television Centre had suddenly vanished into thin air the watching spectators could hardly have been more surprised than they were when Paddington suddenly emerged from the building and hurried across the forecourt with a determined expression on his face.

A hush fell over everyone as he clambered over the top of the sandbags; a hush that was only equalled by the cheer which went up a moment or so later when he reappeared clutching the suitcase. Holding it up for all to see, he started to unload it.

"Blimey!" said a voice in the crowd, as Paddington picked up a white object and placed it into his mouth. "I've never seen anything like this before. I reckon 'e deserves a medal."

"Hear! Hear!" agreed someone else. "The M.B.E. at least."

"More like the D.C.M. if you ask me," murmured John Noakes as he and the rest of the Blue Peter team joined in the general rush to congratulate Paddington. "*Don't Come Monday!* That's the first time I've ever seen anyone defuse a marmalade sandwich!"

"What's he holding up?" gasped Lesley as they drew near. "It looks like an alarm clock."

"It *is* an alarm clock, Miss Judd," said Paddington, pleased to see a familiar face at long last. He shook the object in his paw and then held it up to his ear. "Only I don't think it's working any more," he added sadly. "It must have stopped ticking when I picked it up."

"It was really meant to be a present for Mr O'Donnelly," he explained. "He's having trouble timing his races, so I thought he might like it for when he gives the results next time."

"There's no answer to that," said Peter, breaking the silence which followed as everybody digested this latest piece of information.

"Do you mean to say," began one of the Commissionaires, "that the whole of the Television Centre has been disrupted because of a bear's marmalade sandwich and a dud alarm clock?"

"Don't worry," said John, coming to Paddington's rescue. "I know one programme that's never been put off the air yet, and it won't be today – not if we hurry.

Besides," he took the alarm clock from Paddington and examined it thoughtfully. "I've just had an idea. Has it ever struck anyone," he continued, "how many old alarm clocks there must be lying around in cupboards all over the country – just waiting to be disposed of?"

"There must be thousands and thousands," said Lesley.

"Full of brass cogs," added John.

"At least ten or a dozen in each," agreed Peter, as he began to realise what was in John's mind. "Not to mention all the other bits and pieces."

"There's gold in them thar works," said John. He turned back to Paddington. "We're always on the look-out for things to collect. It may not be much use for Desmond O'Donnelly any more, but it could be an idea for one of our future Appeals."

"And at least the BBC have tested their alarm system," broke in Lesley. "We all know what to do now if there was a real bomb."

"That's all very well," broke in the taxi-driver as he pushed his way to the front of the crowd. "But what about my fare? That's what I'd like to know. I reckon I could do with an appeal being launched for me. Paid me in match-sticks 'e did. *And* there's all me waiting time."

John felt in his pocket. "Have this one on Blue Peter," he said to Paddington. "One way and another I think we've all had our money's worth today, and after all, as the man said: 'none but the brave deserve the fare!'"

When John's remark had been explained to him even Paddington joined in the groans.

"I think," he announced, not to be outdone, "I'd like to clock in at the Television Centre every day of the week!"

HARGREAVES

If you spend half the year hibernating in a box of straw, you tend to get a bit left out of things. So we were delighted when Freda, our Blue Peter tortoise, received a special invitation.

It was not only a great honour to be invited to Oxford University, it was the first time Freda had worn her racing colours and competed against tortoises from all over Britain. The race was in aid of Charity and this is what happened on 1 May 1974.

FREDA'S RACE

10.55 a.m. Crowds had gathered in the courtyard of Corpus Christi College – scene of the South Oxford Regional Tortoise Racing Championships. The official Starter, David Brand, checked Freda's credentials.

11.00 a.m. They're Off! Freda was in lane 5 with me behind her urging her on. Of her six opponents, Fred from Oriel College presented the stiffest opposition.

11.10 a.m. A little gentle persuasion. After a magnificent start Freda gave up. To try and encourage her I switched on some soothing music and a sun lamp. Meanwhile, Fred from Oriel streaked ahead and won with a clear lead of two metres.

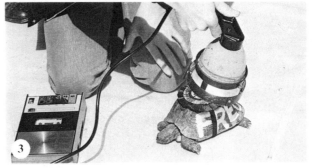

11.45 a.m. The Gallant Loser! Although Freda came last, she had a splendid consolation prize – a golden apple – and a certificate signed by the Keeper of the College Tortoise.

And as she'd never won a prize before – or been to a University – for Freda it was a very successful day!

35

"IT WAS YOUR IDEA-PETE"

On a busy programme like Blue Peter, it's absolutely impossible for one person to have all the ideas. A lot of them come from your letters, anyway; some are from the producers and directors, and some from Val, John, Lesley and me. When it's a hard day's filming in rotten weather, we sometimes look at the director and say "Whose idea *was* this, anyway?" But on the toughest day that I've ever had on Blue Peter, I didn't ask that question – because the answer would have come winging back from an exhausted crew, up to their thighs in mud – *"Yours!"*

Shrimping. It doesn't sound very hard does it? Not when you think of climbing Black Crag – surfing in winter – or mountain rescues in the snow. A nice, gentle, interesting day on the beach – that's what we all *thought* we were in for.

"You'll all need to bring waders," said Brendan Sellick, "because there's quite a bit of mud at this time of the year."

That, we discovered later, was one of the understatements of the century. But we were still enjoying the idyllic scene as we strode across the firm shingle in our new, thigh-length boots.

"We usually wear shorts in the summer, but the mud is so cold in winter time."

It was a bright, sunny, winter's day, and we could see the nets clearly in rows along the horizon. The sun bounced off the still, flat lake of gleaming mud.

"How long will it take us to get there, Brendan?"

"Not long, I hope. You see – in two and a half hours those nets will have 15 metres of water on them, so we can't afford to waste time."

About 90 metres down the beach, the mud began. It was quite shallow to begin with, about ankle deep, although even then it was quite tenacious, and made a satisfying, sucking, slurping sound at every pace.

A little farther on we came to the mud horses. No one knows who first called these strange mud sledges "horses", but Brendan said his great-great-grandfather would have used the same kind of contraption. I wouldn't be surprised if they went back to Roman times. We rolled away the rocks that Brendan leaves on runners to anchor them down against the surge of the incoming tide, and began the long push to the nets.

The mud horses are the shrimpers' wheelbarrows, used for carrying their catch from the nets to the

These are the strange sledges called "mud horses".

No one knows who first invented them, but I reckon they go back to the Romans.

boiling house ashore. The wooden runner underneath is curved at the front like a sledge, and runs so smoothly that even the heaviest load will never bog it down. Once I got going I found putting my whole weight on the handles helped to go faster.

"They go quite well, don't they?" called Brendan. "When it comes a bit hard, dig your toes in and away you'll go."

It came a bit hard about 90 metres farther on. I dug my toes in as Brendan had suggested, but the promise of "away you'll go" didn't seem to be working for my

Gradually I got my breath back, and squelched off along Brendan's tracks to join him at the nets. There were nearly 100 nets set in a long line. Each one was funnel-shaped, and as the ebb tide rushes back through them, the shrimps get caught in the ends. And not only the shrimps! There were plaice, sole, bass and mullet – even eels – all mixed up together in the bulging nets. Brendan sells off the larger fish to the local fishmonger, and the small ones go to the Slimbridge Wildfowl Trust to feed the birds.

But it was the shrimps we were after. It was a good

I was up to my knees in mud, my heart was pounding against my ribs and I thought I was stuck for ever!

By the low-water mark there were about 100 funnel-shaped nets.

Brendan gave me a basket and told me to empty the nets.

mud horse. The mud got deeper and deeper and I got slower and slower. The pain in my calves stretched up to my thighs. My back was breaking and my heart pounded against my ribs like a sledge-hammer. I knew I just couldn't move another step.

"Would somebody take this one over, please?" I heard myself saying above my deafening heart beat.

I trailed on, mud horseless, behind 50-year-old Brendan and Adrian and Nigel, who were pounding away towards the nets and actually *chatting* as they went. After ten more agonising paces, I just gave up and sat down where I was in a metre of stinking mud! I was well beyond caring.

The narrow end was packed solid with hundreds of grey shrimps.

And not only shrimps! The big fish are sold to the local fishmonger.

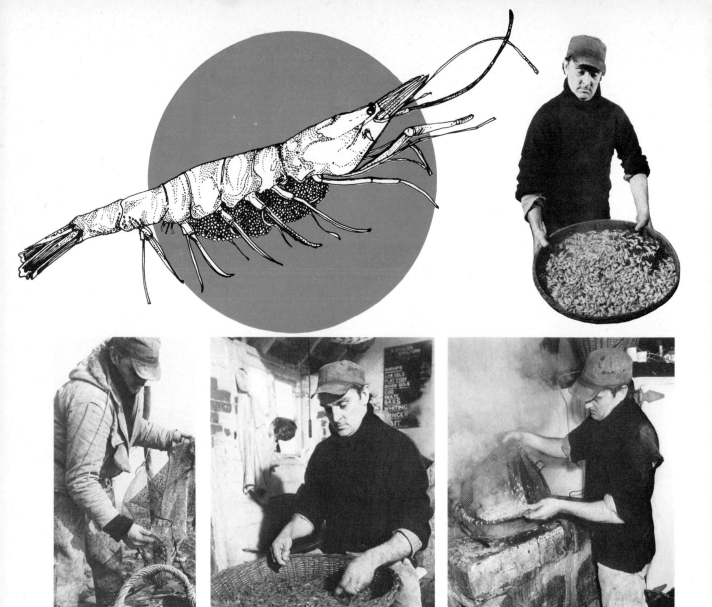

Back ashore at the boiling house, the whole family joins in for the final sorting of the catch.

The shrimps are a dull grey colour before they are boiled, which turns them into the familiar pink you see in the shops.

It took us six hours to catch and boil 70 lbs of shrimps. From now on, every time I eat a shrimp I'll remember the back-breaking mud flats of Stolford.

catch, and we were able to fill our mud horses to the brim. Brendan had reset all his nets and was ready for the journey back, but we wanted to take one or two more shots for the film.

"Don't be too long now, will you?" said Brendan looking out towards the sea. "That tide won't wait for anyone – not even the BBC!"

I'd been so busy with the shrimps I hadn't noticed that the roar of the oncoming surf was growing ominously louder. I remembered what Brendan said about the nets being covered in 15 metres of water, and began the long trudge back to the shore. I didn't collapse that time. With the roaring tide ringing in my ears, I didn't need another incentive!

All the shrimps in the mud horses were a dull, grey colour. It's not until they're boiled that they turn pink, and boiling is part of the fisherman's job. The whole family, including a very fat cat, were waiting in the boiler-house to help with the final sorting. We loaded mountains of grey shrimps into the huge copper boiler. The air was filled with steam and an overpowering smell of cooking shrimps.

It took us just over six hours to catch and boil 70 pounds of shrimps. It was the hardest day's work I've ever done, and whenever I eat a shrimp from now on, I'll remember the Sellick family and the gleaming stinking, back-breaking mud flats of Stolford.

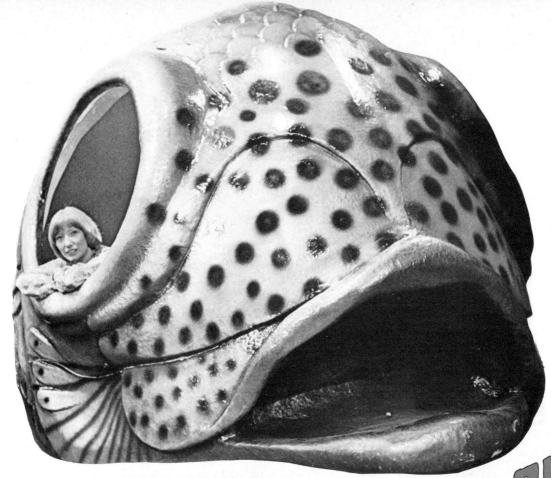

'THE SEA WE WOULD LIKE TO SEE' BLUE PETER EXPO '75 COMPETITION

That's the theme of Expo '75, and this is how our Expo '75 competition began – with a studio full of deep sea monsters and giant fish.

Three weeks later, we had another studio full of weird and fantastic watery creatures – ones that had been created by Blue Peter viewers. Our competition produced a staggering 182,000 drawings and paintings – not only showing strange fish, but plans for underwater cities, anti-pollution devices, and new marine inventions.

The Top Prize Winners came to the studio with their paintings – all of which are being exhibited at Expo itself, together with 50 of the top runners-up. And another 300 of the runners-up have gone to Tokyo for a Special Exhibition at the Tokyo Metropolitan Children's House.

Over-all winner of the competition was 14-year-old Alistair Paterson of Wirral, Merseyside. Alistair's beautiful symbolic circular painting called "Man in Harmony with the Sea" won him a 12-day trip to Japan as a guest of the Japanese Government & Tourist Board.

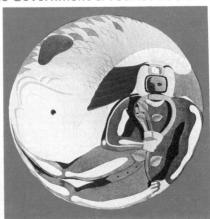

You'd like to paint a picture? You don't know what to draw? Your troubles are over! Make yourself a Spinning Picture Machine like mine and become an instant artist.

It's run by a 4½ or 6 volt electric motor. If you've got one from an old model, you're in luck, but even if you decide to buy one, this gadget is still a money saver. You can use it to make postcards, birthday cards, pictures of all kinds, and every single one will come out different! As well as the motor, this is what you will need:

A 4½ volt "flat" electric battery.
2 pieces of insulated connecting wire 25–35 cm long.
1 piece of wood about
30 x 5 x 2 cm
4 paper clips.
2 small and 3 large rubber bands.
1 rubber. Compasses.
2 8 cm nails.
Corrugated cardboard.
Supply of white paper or card for pictures. Sticky tape.
Old newspapers.
Hammer, small drill, pencil, rubber, glue, scissors.
Poster paints (not too runny!) or felt tipped pens.

SPINNING PICTURES

BASE AND MOTOR:

1. Mark position of 2 nails, 2 cm from end of wood base.

FIG. 1.

2. Drill 2 holes to avoid wood splitting then knock in the 2 nails taking care that they are upright.
3. Fix motor to nails with 2 strong rubber bands.
4. Twist base end of connecting wire to end of each motor lead and cover join with sticky tape.

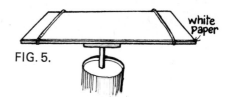

FIG. 2.

Fix paper clips to other ends of connecting wires. Fix flat battery to end of baseboard with strong rubber band and tidy leads with an extra rubber band.

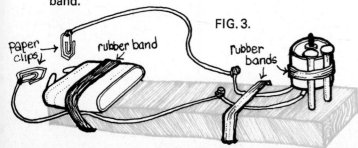

FIG. 3.

SPINNING TABLE:

1. Cut out a postcard (14 x 9 cm) sized piece of cardboard.
2. Draw diagonal lines on card to find the centre point then glue rubber to centre with strong glue.

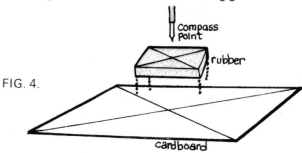

FIG. 4.

3. Stick a compass point in to centre of rubber to make a guide hole.
4. Press rubber gently on to shaft of motor.
5. Cut out piece of white paper (or back of stiff, white Christmas card) the same size as the table and slip on 2 thin rubber bands to keep it in place.

FIG. 5.

6. Spin the table by hand to make sure it is level.

COLLAR:

To stop paint flying around the room make a protective collar from a piece of corrugated cardboard about 90 x 16 cm. Just clip the ends together and cut out a slot to clear the baseboard.

FIG. 6.

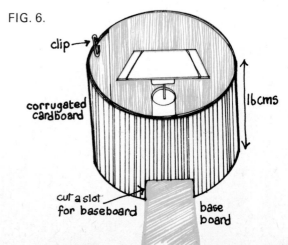

MAKING PICTURES

Hold a felt tipped pen lightly on the spinning table, like I'm doing, or use poster paint mixed to a creamy consistency – rather like thick sauce coming out of a bottle. If it is too liquid there will be a nasty mess and no picture! You could use old squeezy bottles or small plastic cosmetic bottles to hold and squirt the paint. IF YOU CHOOSE PAINT, REMEMBER TO PUT THE CARDBOARD COLLAR ON THE MACHINE.

Place the machine on a double thickness of newspaper. Put a small dollop of paint – enough to cover a 1p piece – near the centre of the white card. Add several similar dollops of other colours. Connect the paper clips to the battery and let the table spin round for about 6 seconds.

PETRA

Petra must surely be television's best-known and best-loved dog. She's been in nearly a thousand different programmes and taken part in hundreds of films, and you've only got to be in the Blue Peter office when the postman arrives on her birthday to know how popular she is with viewers all over Britain.

Christmas 1962 was Petra's first appearance on Blue Peter. Since then – apart from having her puppies – she's never missed a programme.

Petra's eight puppies were born in 1965. Blue Peter viewers chose their names – Rover, Rex, Candy, Kim, Bruce, Peter, Prince and Patch.

Patch was the puppy we decided to keep on the programme, and John looked after him.

Petra made friends with Daniel, the Blue Peter baby. She was always gentle and trustworthy.

All dogs need plenty of exercise and Petra has a good run in the park at least once a day.

Many Happy Returns! On each of her birthdays, Petra receives more cards than a pop star.

She arrived in time for Christmas in 1962. Since then, apart from taking time off to have her puppies, Petra's never missed a programme. She's always been a very reliable dog – an extremely good example of what a great pet an ordinary mongrel can make. And Petra's a real mixture. Sometimes people seeing her on television think she's an Alsatian – but she's not. She's considerably smaller and thinner, and if you saw her next to a true Alsatian, you'd notice the difference immediately. We haven't a clue what her background is, but she's highly intelligent, responded well to her training when she was a puppy – she even won a certificate at her obedience class – and has always been gentle and even-tempered.

There's just one exception – Petra hates dark trousers. We think this goes back to an early experience she found rather frightening. A brass band came to the Blue Peter studio – Petra hadn't heard one before, and had the shock of her life when a trombone suddenly blasted off, right behind her left ear.

The bandsmen were all wearing dark blue trousers, and like an elephant, Petra's never forgotten. This has led to some awkward moments with our visitors – especially the time when she growled and bared her teeth at a group of very friendly policemen who'd come to put on a display. What's more, Petra's always disliked the studio where the brass band incident took place – it just shows how important early influences can be.

From the time she first appeared on the programme as a tiny puppy, Petra's always had lots of fan mail. Her name was chosen for her by Blue Peter viewers who sent in thousands of suggestions. She always receives as many birthday cards and presents as a pop star, and when her puppies were born in 1965, she even had telegrams of congratulations.

Petra's eight pups were born at half past three in the afternoon of Thursday, 9 September. It was an exciting moment because we'd always hoped she'd have some. The pups' father was Moss, a Shetland Sheepdog, and there were seven dogs and one bitch.

All eight were fit and healthy, and Petra was a marvellous mother. Having a large family didn't seem to bother her at all, and when we decided to keep one of the litter – a smooth-coated, light-haired dog with a small light patch on his forehead – Petra helped with his training. Patch soon became as well known as Petra, and when John joined the programme, Patch became his dog.

On 22 November 1966 Petra had her first grand-puppies, Brandy, Dandy and Mandy. And a year later, she became a great-grandmother when Zebedee and Zabadak were born.

Some of her pups are still alive – one of them, Candy, has emigrated to Canada, but of course, one thing that all owners have to reckon with is that pets don't live nearly as long as human beings. It was a sad moment for all of us when Petra's son, Patch, died in 1971. It was very sudden and unexpected, but we did at least know we'd looked after him as well as we possibly could.

Petra's an old lady now, and like elderly humans, she's not as quick as she was, and she's having to take life more easily. We've discovered, too, that she has a very rare form of diabetes, which means she has to have special care taken of her. But she's not in any kind of pain and still loves to run in the park, so we're doing all we can to make her happy.

As far as we're concerned, there'll never be another dog like Petra!

London's streets are full of romance. Strange things have happened in the buildings that line them. Wimpole Street, for instance, is a busy street in London's West End. Many of the houses are doctors' consulting rooms because this is the heart of the smart medical quarter.

The Runaways

In the last century, these were family houses, and at Number 50 something happened that was to make the family who lived there the talk of London's High Society.

A daughter of the house ran away to a rendezvous outside St Marylebone Parish Church to meet a fascinating and fashionable man. Such scandalous behaviour was unheard of, and

from that day to this, that family is remembered. They were the "Barretts of Wimpole Street". The daughter's name was Elizabeth, and this is her story.

1 Elizabeth Barrett was an invalid, too weak to leave the house. Her maid Wilson looked after her, and her best friend was Flush, her golden spaniel.

2 He finished Elizabeth's dinner when she did not want her father to know how little she'd eaten.

3 Every evening, Edward Barrett visited Elizabeth. He would talk earnestly and read the Bible. "You are the dearest of my children," he said.

4 On Sundays, Elizabeth's seven brothers and two sisters came to see her. They, too, led dreary lives for Mr Barrett would not allow any of his children to marry or to break away from home.

5 Elizabeth spent her lonely days reading and writing poems. One was about Flush. Her poetry was published, so although poor Miss Barrett never left the house, she had become quite famous and many people wrote to her.

6 One man wrote again and again, begging to be allowed to see her. He was Robert Browning, a young poet. At last, Elizabeth wrote to him and said "Yes".

7 Robert and Elizabeth became friends. They talked of books and foreign lands, especially Italy. His energy and love of life made her feel stronger, too.

8 For the first time in years, Elizabeth felt strong enough to leave the house. Her delighted sisters took her out in a bath chair, while Mr Barrett looked on with disapproval.

9 Soon she could take Flush for walks in nearby Regent's Park. He barked excitedly – this was better than lying on a sofa while Elizabeth wrote poetry to him!

10 Robert Browning loved Elizabeth very much. ''Marry me,'' he begged. Elizabeth knew her father would forbid her, and that if she left with Robert, he would not allow her to see her brothers and sisters again. But at last, Elizabeth agreed to marry at the end of the summer.

11 In September, Robert sent a letter. From the envelope dropped three dead leaves, a sign that summer was over. Elizabeth was in despair. She loved Robert and wanted to marry – yet how could she leave her family for ever?

12 Then a blow fell. Mr. Barrett suddenly announced that he was closing 50 Wimpole Street. All the family must move to the country, and Elizabeth must come, too. ''He's doing it to stop me seeing Robert,'' thought Elizabeth, aghast. Now her mind was made up!

13 One Saturday morning, Elizabeth and Robert met secretly at St Marylebone Parish Church and with only the faithful Wilson in attendance, Elizabeth Barrett married Robert Browning.

14 After the ceremony, two carriages were waiting, and the bride and bridegroom, without a word, each got into one and drove away.

15 Back in her lonely room in Wimpole Street, Elizabeth wore Robert's ring on a ribbon round her neck. Her father visited her as usual, but she dared not tell him she was married. Only Flush and Wilson knew.

16 She stayed there a week, whilst Robert made arrangements for them to go away together. As Elizabeth wrote farewell letters to all her family, Wilson secretly packed her luggage.

17 At last, a week after the wedding day, Elizabeth, Flush and the faithful Wilson crept out of the silent house. She was an invalid no longer. She was Mrs Robert Browning, off to live a new life in the colour and excitement of Italy.

aMAZEing

Working on Blue Peter, you meet some strange people who do even stranger things for a living. But I think Greg Bright has the most peculiar occupation I've ever come across.

He's a MAZE maker! It's a fact — he spends all his time making mazes of every shape and size. Not only has he painted and drawn hundreds of mazes (his Bournemouth design covers 26 square metres) but on Good Friday in 1971 he seized a spade and dug one with his bare hands out of the earth. It took him over a year to complete, and when he had finished, it was the biggest earth maze in the world. It covers two-thirds of an acre and runs for well over a mile. An eighth of the trenches are two metres deep, the rest vary between half a metre and a metre.

Four years later, I went back with Greg to the site of the Great Pilton maze, as it had become known. It had completely disappeared. Huge grasses and reeds had grown up and totally engulfed Greg's masterwork. I felt so sorry for him, I hardly knew what to say, but Greg didn't bat an eyelid.

"We'd better get a couple of bill-hooks and start hacking," he said.

"But that'll take a lifetime," I said, looking at the great jungle of reeds.

"It shouldn't take me as long as building it," he replied nonchalantly, "and anyway, I've got you to help me."

I found the start of the trench quite easily — by falling two metres through the grass into 60 cms of muddy water. I looked up and saw Greg's head silhouetted against the sky.

"That's the spot where I put the first spade in," he said, nostalgically.

As we began our mammoth task of hacking down the undergrowth, I asked him if he started by making a design on paper.

"No — I just drew with my spade on the earth," he said. "I'd no plan in my head at all. Then after a week's digging, my ideas began to form."

During his dig, Greg lived alone in a tent in the centre of the field. In that year, he reckoned he moved two thousand cubic feet of earth.

We hacked our way slowly to the middle. I realised that when Greg was digging it, he wouldn't have been able to see where he was going because the trenches were well above his head. The amazing thing is that without any kind of plan he managed to create a beautiful, fluid maze. Beautiful is right, because when seen from the air, the design is an absolute delight.

It took us hours and hours of hacking to reveal the maze, and then, because our filming time was running out, I cheated and hired some local labour to help us finish it off.

At last we stood triumphant at the centre point and looked across the field at the extraordinary swirls and patterns of Greg's handiwork. I was exhausted from just doing the clearing job, but I was quite bowled over when I thought of the extraordinary tenacity and determination needed to dig two thousand cubic metres of earth single-handed.

"Did you ever feel despairing when you were doing it?" I asked Greg.

"Oh yes, frequently," he said smiling.

"You must be very keen indeed on mazes," I said admiringly.

"Oh no," he replied. "I hate them."

As I said at the beginning — you do meet some extraordinary people working on Blue Peter!

The End of a Dream

In the corner of the airfield at Cardington in Bedfordshire there still stands the enormous empty hangar where the R 101 was built. The huge, echoing, empty building is all that remains of Britain's hope to lead the world in the conquest of the skies by airship.

The R 101 was to be the greatest and the most luxurious airship ever invented, and in 1929, airships were the most revolutionary form of transport. The huge, silver cigar-shaped balloon, filled with hydrogen gas, could carry a passenger car which was more like a flying hotel than an aeroplane. In place of tight-packed rows of seats and trays of warmed up food in today's jets, there were lounges, bedrooms, Palm Courts, and dining-rooms laid out with gleaming silver.

A great army of technicians worked ceaselessly in the hangar at Cardington. The zero date was 4 October 1930. She must be ready by then for the grand inaugural flight to India. Many VIPs had already been invited.

"It's too soon," said the experts. "She won't be ready in time." But the Government officials would have none of it. Lord Thomson, the Air Minister, waved all the objections aside.

"She'll be as safe as houses," he declared.

A young man named Commander Atherstone, who had won the Air Force Cross for his work on airships during World War I, was a member of the Cardington team. He was a great airship enthusiast, but he, too, was worried that the R 101 was not going to be ready in time.

Ten months before the maiden flight, he wrote in his diary: "We have not made a single flight in which something or other has not broken down."

But like the rest of the team, he pressed on. Every morning he would arrive at the great hangar with Timmy, his Alsatian dog, at his heels. And on every test flight, Timmy would wait faithfully by the mooring post for the airship to return, bringing his master home.

The days raced by. On 3 October, Commander Atherstone wrote in his diary: "Everybody is so keyed up now, as we all feel that the future of airships depends on what kind of show we put up. Let's hope for good luck and do our best."

At 7.00 p.m. on 4 October 1930, in a glare of publicity, the R 101 finally left her mooring mast at Cardington with 54 passengers and crew on board: destination – India.

After crossing the channel and making her way steadily over the French coast, the captain sent this message: "At the moment, the passengers, after an excellent meal and a number of cigars, are getting ready for bed."

Young Commander Atherstone, after a hectic day, would probably have already been asleep.

It was 1.50 a.m. when disaster struck. The great airship crashed into a low hill near Beauvais in France and immediately burst into flames. The hydrogen gas that kept the ship

airborne, turned the fire into a raging inferno. The blaze could be seen ten miles away. Out of the 54 people on board there were only 7 survivors. Lord Thomson, who had been so confident, perished with young Commander Atherstone.

The whole world was shattered and stunned by the news. Britain mourned not only for the victims of the disaster, but the death of the whole idea of travel by airship.

Amongst the mourners was Timmy the Alsatian, who waited every day by the mooring mast for Commander Atherstone's return. At last, realising he would never see his master again, Timmy died of grief.

FOOTNOTE:
When the tragic story of the R 101 was first shown on Blue Peter,

Rebecca Jones, an assistant on John Craven's News Round, caught a glimpse of it on the screen as she was waiting to put Newsround on the air. She rang the Blue Peter office and told us that her grandfather, Commander Atherstone, had been on the R 101 and had kept a meticulously accurate diary of the events that led up to the great disaster. The next week, she brought the diary to the studio and showed it on the programme.

Rebecca is a pretty blonde of 25 and, of course, could never have known her grandfather.

"But we all feel very proud of him," she told John as she looked again at the last words he ever wrote:

"Let's hope for good luck and do our best."

should be able to get away with about 28 tons of fuel on board which should give us nearly 100% reserve. Everybody is rather keyed up now, as we all feel that the future of airships very largely depends on what sort of a show we put up. There are very many unknown factors and I feel that that thing called 'Luck' will figure rather conspicuously in our flight. Let's hope for good luck and do our best!

EXTRACT FROM LIEUT. COMMANDER ATHERSTONE'S JOURNAL

The R101 Crashes And Is Destroyed: Lord Thomson, Sir Sefton Brancker And 44 Others Burned To Death.

Key to numbers.

1. Huge 777-foot-long, cigar-shaped body or "envelope" made up of aluminium lattice-work girders and covered with fabric. **2.** Gas bags containing the hydrogen gas which kept the ship aloft. **3.** Five power cars suspended beneath the envelope propelled the R101 at a speed of over 60 m.p.h. Each contained a 650-horsepower Beardmore diesel engine which drove a large variable-pitch propeller, constantly attended by an engineer who gained access to the car by ladder. The small propeller on the front drove a generator for electricity. **4.** Reinforced nose section containing the mooring gear. At the very tip was a mooring eye by which the airship was attached to its mast, and above was the bow look-out position. **5.** Drop-down gangway by which passengers and crew entered the ship. **6.** The tail end or stern look-out position. **7.** Crew's gangways running the full length of the ship. **8.** Rudders and elevator planes for steering and manoeuvring the ship. **9.** Two decks cradled beneath the gas bags ran the full width of the ship to provide space for 35 crew members and up to 100 passengers. Walls were made of canvas and panelled in balsa wood to save weight. Furniture was made of lightweight wicker-work (painted green to fit in with the cream-and-gold overall colour scheme). **10.** Twin berth passenger cabins. (More were situated on the lower deck.) **11.** Dining saloon seating 50 passengers. **12.** Passengers' lounge. **13** and **14.** Promenade decks, fitted with large observation windows from which passengers could look down on the scenery over which they were passing. **15.** Washing and toilet spaces. **16.** Smoke room — the only place on the airship where smoking was allowed due to the fire risk caused by the explosive nature of hydrogen gas. **17.** The galley where meals were prepared on electric cooking ranges. **18.** Pantry and food store. **19.** Crew's sleeping and living space. **20.** Wireless cabin. **21.** The chart room where the ship's course was plotted by the navigator. **22.** The control car, suspended beneath the ship and from where it was steered. In the control car stood the captain in full command of his vessel. **23.** Passengers' access gangway leading up to the nose of the ship. **24.** A compensating tank. These were dotted about the ship and were filled with diesel fuel oil to maintain trim when few or no passengers were carried.

R101

Halfway between a flying hotel and an ocean liner, the largest airship in the world was to have been the last word in sky travel, linking Britain with her Empire by air.

A peep behind the curtained door of a passenger cabin. Each cabin had two bunks, and warm air wafted up through a grille in the floor.

Swinging at anchor above the Bedfordshire countryside. Mooring towers were built at stopping points along the route to India to be taken by R 101.

OPERATION SPRING CLEAN

I'll never forget the day I spring cleaned this eagle. Perched high on The Natural History Museum, Europe's largest terracotta building, it was having its first wash for nearly a hundred years.

The Natural History Museum is one of London's most impressive buildings, and when I discovered it was covered with scaffolding, I thought I'd investigate. A team of five men who'd been working on the cleaning operation for no less than nine and a half months were on their last lap when I arrived, and when I'd been fitted out with my cleaning kit, I started my long climb up to the West Tower's top-most pinnacle. It was a strange sensation coming face to face with a dirty eagle, 80 metres above the roar of London's traffic. After almost a hundred years in the open, the stone was covered with layers of grimy grease. A special de-greaser had to be sprayed on, left for a few minutes and then sprayed off with a high-pressure water jet. The next stage was of vital importance. A chemical containing 2% of hydrochloric acid was brushed on and left for an hour. Next came the high-pressure hose again — and like a conjuring trick — the dirt fell off and my eagle was as good as new.

The museum's 200-metre frontage was covered with a network of scaffolding and interconnecting ladders.

Gargoyles like these aren't just for decoration. Inside they contain drainage troughs and pipes to stop the rain damaging the walls.

The Natural History museum dates back over 200 years. The original collection was housed on the present site of the British Museum, but it wasn't really very convenient. Tickets had to be written for in advance and visitors were limited to 10 people for 3 hours per day – they were conducted by a guide and not allowed to pause in front of the cases. But in 1860 it was decided that the Natural History Department needed more space, so Alfred Waterhouse was commissioned to design a new museum. It was to be the first terracotta building of its time, and it's still the

Another view the public doesn't usually see – a whole line up of gargoyles looking like guardsmen on parade.

largest terracotta building in Europe, with about 200 metres of frontage and 80 metres high at the towers. It was opened in 1881 and Alfred Waterhouse's original drawings are still kept in the Museum basement.

Architect Alfred Waterhouse chose blue and buff terracotta for his museum, not only because it looked nice, but also because he thought it was the material most likely to withstand the city's pollution. He was right. Underneath a century's dirt, the stone is incredibly well preserved.

My eagle wasn't the only terracotta creature that had to be cleaned. The museum's decorated with hundreds of them and they weren't built just to look nice. For instance, down one ladder I found a gargoyle looking rather like a cat. When I peered inside I found a trough lined with lead. At the base, two drainage pipes flow into the trough, then along and out through the mouth – in this way the rainwater doesn't pour down the terracotta surface of the building and cause damage.

The 2½ million annual visitors to the Museum probably remember the huge models and skeletons, like the fishes, sharks and dinosaurs, best of all – like the skeleton of a Diplodocus, the largest four-footed animal which ever lived. This prehistoric Diplodocus was 26 metres long and probably weighed 50 tons, but in spite of his size he wasn't at all fierce. His brain was about the size of a chicken's egg and he lived off plants, an easy prey for the meat-eating dinosaurs around at that time, 150 million years ago.

No one has ever seen a living Diplodocus – they died out long before the earliest men – but by careful study of fossilised skeletons, experts have pieced together information about the way they lived. To protect himself from the land dinosaurs, Diplodocus spent most of his life in shallow waters. His huge clawed feet helped him to walk in the slippery

Inside, the Museum houses one of the two biggest natural history collections in the world, with over 100,000 specimens on show. The first exhibit in the main entrance hall is a display of the largest land mammals. They aren't models – they're stuffed, and they're very life-like!

This skeleton of a Diplodocus is 26 metres long, including 7 metres of neck and 15 of tail. He weighed about 50 tons and lived 150 million years ago.

In spite of his size, the Diplodocus wasn't fierce. His brain was roughly the size of a chicken's egg and he lived off plants, not meat.

mud and his long neck – 7 metres of it – made it easy for him to reach food while still safely away from the bank. The water also helped to support his massive weight.

Of course, a great deal of his length was in his tail – 15 metres long. And even with that he wasn't the largest creature who's ever lived on earth. That honour belongs to an animal who's far from extinct – the Blue Whale.

With the Museum looking so smart inside, I was pleased to see the outside being transformed. And when it's all finished, the restored Natural History Museum will be Britain's biggest contribution to European Architectural Heritage Year.

Each year we try and put on a mini spectacular for our Christmas programme – like being the ugly sisters with Arthur Askey, or learning to dance the back legs of a pantomime horse. Last Christmas we presented our "Blue Peter Flying Ballet". And here's how it turned out to be just about the most uncomfortable few hours in the history of man-powered flight!

"You've jumped five miles out of an aeroplane," we said to John – "You do it."

"You can't have a Flying Ballet with just one flyer," he replied. "Let's all do it."

How we wished we hadn't!

It's all very well going to pantomimes and shows like Peter Pan, and seeing the actors and actresses swooping effortlessly over the stage and high above the auditorium with the grace and ease of birds. Wearing costumes that transform the flyers into witches, butterflies or astronauts, most of the audience don't realise they're all trussed up like chickens ready for the oven, with complicated harnesses that cut into arms and legs and pull in the most awkward directions. And it's unbelievable that a flight that lasts less than two minutes on the stage can take literally weeks of rehearsals to perfect.

We were in trouble right from the start. First of all, with all the other things to prepare for the programmes,

we didn't have time for weeks of rehearsals, not even days. We grabbed a quick three hours and hoped for the best. And that's why our Blue Peter ballet wasn't exactly classical – with all its mid-air collisions.

But at least we *did* get airborne – and that was all due to our friend Eric Dunning who's been teaching actors and actresses to fly on stage and screen for close on 15 years.

Thanks to Eric, we didn't have any really bad accidents and we learned quite a lot about the way flying ballets began.

It seems that actors flew over the stage at Drury Lane as long ago as 1760. They actually carried blazing torches as they swooped over the audience, so it's hardly surprising the theatre was burned down several times.

But Eric thinks that stage flying originated in Germany where large and cumbersome machinery was used, which was difficult to move about.

Over the years, the equipment has become smaller and more sophisticated, and can be adapted to TV and film studios as well as theatres.

In spite of the way the equipment's changed, it's still necessary to have one operator per flyer. It's the operator who controls vital things like the line of flight, elevation and the landings. He has to work hand-in-glove with his flyer – and all the moves have to be rehearsed to split-second timing.

Flying expert, Eric Dunning, helped to fit my complicated canvas and nylon harness. Strong wire cables attached to the harness went through a series of pulleys in the studio roof.

To reach my "take off" point – the top of our studio shelves – Peter and Eric gave me a helping hand. My line of flight had to be carefully planned to avoid a mid-air collision.

John gave a demonstration of how it works before we performed our ballet and Eric was his teacher. Four metres from where John was perched on top of our studio shelves, the operator held on to his rope. This was connected to a geared machine, and then attached to a strong wire cable that went through a system of pulleys high up in our studio roof. It's this flexible cable that was linked to the harness John wore under his shirt. The wires were so fine they were almost invisible, and the harness itself, although lightweight, was very, very strong – a mixture of canvas and nylon, and covered in straps and buckles. When the rope was pulled, John

Eric guided me through the air as – four metres away – an operator pulled on my rope. This was attached via a geared machine to the wire cables.

From upside down in mid-air, the Blue Peter Studio looked quite different! My flying wires were so thin they were almost invisible.

Learning to land was very difficult, and mastering the technique of somersaulting and flying upside down was even harder.

For the Blue Peter Flying Ballet, John and Peter – dressed as giant budgies – were released from their cage by good fairies Val and Lesley.

After the budgies had stretched their wings and tried to fly, we all had to line up for a final bow. Not at all easy when you're hovering in mid-air!

"flew" from the top of the shelf and across the studio. Landing's quite difficult until you've been able to practise a few times, and learning to somersault and fly upside down are even harder.

Once you're in your harness and wired up, you can only fly in certain directions according to where the flying equipment's been fixed in the studio roof, and the more people there are flying, the more complicated this is to arrange. The whole thing has to be choreographed like an ordinary ballet – only when you fly, people's lives are at stake.

Eric warned us there'd been one or two fatal accidents, and this was easy to believe. In actual flight you move quite speedily – and as it would look a bit odd if a corps de flying ballet wore crash helmets, all the pre-flight planning is of supreme importance. Eric said the most difficult tricks he'd ever had to arrange were for some of the James Bond films, and the space film "2001". But without doubt the quickest flying he'd arranged was for

Blue Peter. Within three hours he'd given us all lessons, and sorted out our sequences. John and Pete – dressed in two enormous yellow budgie costumes with huge budgie heads and feet – had to fly around their cage and play with their budgie mirror and bell. Val and Lesley, dressed as fairies, with wands and wings, took pity on the budgies and flew to rescue them.

After making the cage disappear, the fairies helped the budgies stretch their wings and then we all lined up, hovering 3 metres off the ground to take a final bow. There was music, too, to add to the confusion – but in the end, we all managed to finish together.

Eric said if only there'd been time, we would have become quite good. But as we undressed and looked at our grazed shins and bruised thighs and arms where we'd bumped into each other – or the scenery – we thought once was quite enough. From now on, flying's strictly for the birds – or Peter Pan!

THE DAY THE "GASKETS BLEW"

The day was Friday, 4 October. The place was an engine shed at Neville Hill, Leeds. The time was 3.30 in the afternoon, and the sight a pretty depressing one! There was the 532 Blue Peter with steam pouring out in all the wrong directions – and only 18 hours to go before she was due to make her first proper journey under steam since she left service with British Rail way back in 1966. All that could be done was to damp down the fire, wait for the boiler to cool, and for her volunteer engineers to work all night, hoping to get the damage repaired in time to meet the schedule.

Amazingly, the job got done and on Saturday, 5 October, 532 Blue Peter steamed out of Neville Hill precisely on time. On the foot-plate was Driver Harry Neal, and I joined him at Nomanton to give a hand with the stoking.

The Blue Peter is a strong, powerful engine, though not exactly a race-horse. But she was reaching speeds of 40 m.p.h. in spite of the dodgy gaskets, and that meant shovelling 3½ tons of coal into the firebox to keep up a good head of steam. It was hot work, but well worth while. All along the line, hundreds of Blue Peter viewers turned out to give us a wave. Then, 120 miles after leaving Leeds, Blue Peter steamed triumphantly into Tyseley. Not a single thing had gone wrong. The gaskets had held and she'd arrived spot on time to go on show at the Birmingham Steam Museum. Now she's back in Yorkshire and after that first successful run, others may follow. But one place the 532 runs frequently, and with no gasket trouble, is on our Blue Peter layout! Sometimes she runs as a goods train, thanks to John's ingenious idea for do-it-yourself freight.

Freight Train

COAL TRUCK

1 Cut a piece of thin card the same length as the truck and a little wider. Bend the sides to make a little platform which will slot neatly into the truck.

2 Crumble a piece of a polystyrene ceiling tile into granules. Cover the top of the card with rubber solution glue and stick on the granules.

3 When the glue is dry, paint the granules with black poster paint to look like coal.

Make your railway pay by running fully loaded goods trains. Container wagons are expensive, so get empty trucks and fill them yourself with home-made freight. It's a cheap and easy way to add realism to your layout. Here's the freight I've made to be carried by the 532 Blue Peter.

STONE CHIPPINGS

Make a little cardboard platform to fit your wagon in exactly the same way as for the coal truck. This time glue on lentils to cover the top and paint them grey to look like stone.

SHORT PIPES

1 Using your truck as a pattern, cut a piece of card to fit the floor.

2 Glue bits of macaroni to the card in neat rows. Paint them grey or brown to look like drain-pipes.

thin card

fold

ceiling tile

saucer for granules

BLACK PAINT

thin card folded

GLUE

LE

lentils

paint grey

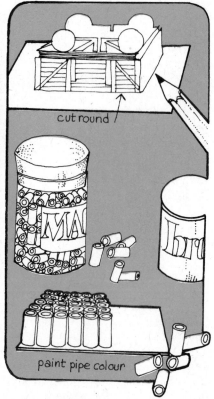

cut round

MAC

bro

paint pipe colour

LONG PIPES

Drinking-straws cut in half make good drain-pipes. Glue the first layer to a piece of thin card, then glue more straws on top to make a full load. When the glue's dry, paint the straws a "pipe" colour.

TIMBER LOAD

Save up ice-lolly sticks and convert them into planks. Trim off the rounded ends and split each stick down the middle to make two planks from each one.

LOG WAGON

Cut garden twigs to the same length as your wagon and to stop them rolling off, glue them to a piece of card. A bit of chain from a broken neck-lace glued over each end of the twigs is a good finishing touch.

cut drinking straws in half

drinki straws

GLUE

view from below

Paint straws

trim off ends

split each stick in half

GLUE

view from below

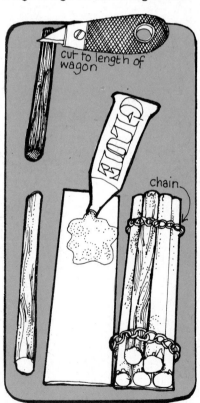

cut to length of wagon

GLUE

chain

THE CASE OF THE MALTESE CROSS

Can you solve this case?
Six careless mistakes gave away the crook.
We spotted them—
Can you?

"... and the Knights of St John loaded their cannons with Turkish heads and fired them back at their tormentors. No mercy was given, since none was expected."

Professor Johnston, expert in Maltese history, took a sip of water as his spellbound audience waited for his lecture to continue.

Detective Inspector McCann had brought his nephew, Bob, to this Saturday-morning lecture at the Institute. At the start, Bob had been very disappointed when the Professor announced that the Grand Gold Cross of St John, which was being specially brought from Malta, had been delayed.

"Mr Fennelon should have been here by now," the Professor had explained, "and I'm afraid something must have happened to him. He's bringing the Cross from Malta specially for an exhibition at the Royal Academy, and I'd hoped he was going to call in here en route to give us a special preview."

Bob had always wanted to see this famed 16th-century jewel that had been the inspiration of the Knights of St John of Malta during the famous siege. However, he soon became so engrossed by Professor Johnston's tales of heroism that it came as quite a shock when the door at the back of the hall burst open and the Professor stopped in mid-sentence. Framed in the doorway between two security guards was a small, dark figure, carrying a red leather case.

"Ladies and Gentlemen," said Professor Johnston, "as you can see, Mr Fennelon has arrived from Malta at last. Come forward so you'll be able to see closely the Order's most priceless relic."

As the audience eagerly gathered round, Bob heard a perspiring Mr Fennelon apologising for his late arrival.

"I am so sorry, Professor," he said breathlessly, "but the journey has been terrible! All the way from Dover, the M1 motorway was jammed solid."

"I thought you were coming by air," said Johnston.

"I originally intended to," explained Fennelon, but the Minestrone wind was blowing so fiercely in the Black Sea that all flights from Malta were cancelled. I had to come by road across the causeway to Sicily."

But the audience weren't interested in Mr Fennelon's excuses. All eyes were fixed expectantly on the red leather case. For a moment, Mr Fennelon's brown, stubby fingers fumbled with the catch. Then a blaze of diamonds and rubies almost blinded them.

"Gosh!" said Bob.

The audience gasped with amazement.

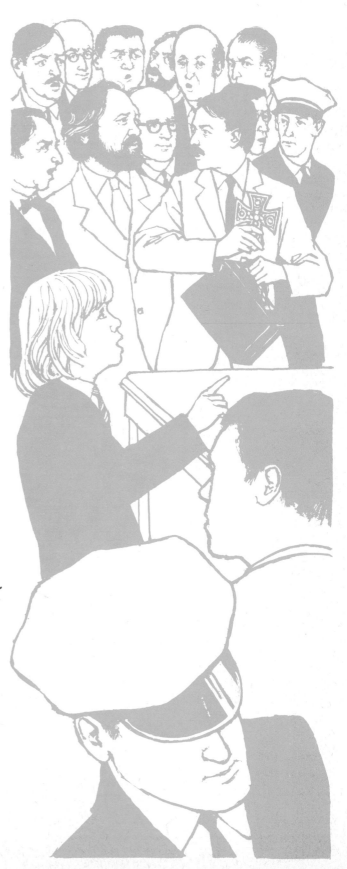

"What do you think of this? It's fantastic, isn't it?" gloated Fennelon. "I bet you've never seen anything like that before!"

"Are those *real* jewels?" said Bob in amazement.

"Of course," cried Fennelon. "The cross is a priceless part of the history of our Island – like the V.C. awarded by His Majesty King George to all the people in Malta who withstood so bravely the second siege in 1940."

Bob's hand reached out to touch the gleaming gems.

"Not to touch, if you please," snapped Mr Fennelon. "I cannot risk any damage to the Cross before it is shown to the public at the Great Siege Exhibition at the National Gallery. And if it is to be in place by six o'clock for the Ambassador's reception, I must leave at once!"

Detective Inspector McCann had been watching silently, but as Fennelon seized the case, he stepped forward.

"I'm afraid you aren't going anywhere for the moment, sir!" he rasped.

"What do you mean?" expostulated the little Maltese.

McCann turned to the security guards.

"When did you first make contact with Mr Fennelon?" he asked.

"Soon as he'd cleared customs, sir," said the burly Sergeant.

"He was late coming through, and didn't seem to expect to be met by security."

"I bet he didn't!" said McCann.

"He didn't seem to want to come here either," said the Guard, "but Professor Johnston had given us our orders, so of course, we carried them out!"

"Bit of luck you did," said McCann.

A telephone shrilled out.

"That," said McCann," unless I'm very much mistaken, will be the Yard telling us they've found the real Mr Fennelon."

"What do you mean, Uncle?" exclaimed Bob.

"It's perfectly simple," McCann assured him. "The real Fennelon must have been overpowered by this impostor, who thought he could get away with the Cross of St John."

"How did you know, Uncle?" said Bob, flabbergasted.

"Six foolish mistakes gave him away," replied McCann, grimly, "and thanks to them, we've prevented a Maltese double cross!"

Did you spot the six clues? Check your answers on page 76.

'IT COULDN'T HAPPEN TO ME'

If you spend a lot of time doing fairly silly things like Pete and I do, you always feel at the back of your mind that accidents are things that happen to other people. Not that we are careless or slap happy. We always take expert advice and observe all the safety precautions. But with all the care in the world, sometimes things go wrong.

However, all those thoughts were far from my mind when I stood by the side of the two-man Bob run in St Moritz, in Switzerland, watching the RAF's bob-sleigh team thundering down the track at 90 mph. I'd only seen it on television before, but I'd always thought that bob-sleighing looked one of the most exciting sports in the world.

A two-man bob has a driver and brakeman. The driver has a left and right control so that he can move the runners and steer the sleigh round the terrifying bends. The brakeman's job is to give the sledge a good push off and then to sit tight and do absolutely nothing until the race is over, when he pulls on the saw tooth brakes which dig into the solid snow, bringing the sleigh to a halt. I thought this didn't sound very important, but Mike Cunningham, the RAF's team leader and crack brakeman, told me he had once got knocked out by a flying piece of ice and wasn't able to apply the brakes.

"We went straight down the run, off through a hedge, across a dual carriageway, over a ploughed field – and stopped just in front of an oak tree!"

The push off is vital if you're going to make a good time. Both men start off on the run, then the driver leaps aboard; as soon as he's secure, the brakeman jumps on the back, swings forward on the push bar, and eases himself into the seat. Once he's settled, he locks himself firmly into the seat by bracing his feet against a bar.

The track has 18 major bends, and each one has a name. There's "Sunny", "Shamrock", "Leap" and "Horseshoe", and one called "Nash & Dixon" named after Britain's last Olympic champions.

John Blockey, who was going to be my driver, thought it would be a good idea for me to "walk" the course with him so that I could have a *slow* look at the run that I'd next see at over 80 mph.

This was my second biggest surprise of the trip. The walls of ice towered over me at more than six metres! When I watched the TV coverage of the champion-ships at home, I'd thought they were about two metres high. I saw runner marks at an unbelievable "wall of death" position about four metres up the sheer ice face.

"Is this where we're going to be?" I asked, hesitantly.

"At this stage, yes," said John. "Of course, we'll be much higher at the top of the bend – so we'll get the maximum acceleration out of the corner. You get about 4G coming round that bend, which means your head will feel about four times its normal weight – so you'll need to brace hard – but we'll get a tremendous kick at the exit!"

"How fast?" I asked.

"About 80 miles an hour, if we're lucky!"

Back at the top, I got kitted up ready for the run. Crash helmet, yellow goggles, anorak, elbow pads, tough leather gloves. I didn't realise at the time, but I was going to be grateful for every layer of protective clothing before the end of the day! I also had a pair of special spiked shoes to give me a grip on the ice. John Blockey gave the soles a last-minute brush to get rid of any snow and ice. I grabbed hard onto the push bar handles and looked across at John, crouched over his cockpit.

"OK John," he said. "We'll rock backwards and forwards on the runners, and I'll call one - a-two - a-three – and then push like hell – OK?"

"OK," I nodded.

"A-one – a-two – a-three!"

My spikes dug into the ice and I pushed with all my might. In one smooth movement, John slid in behind the controls. One – two – onto the platform – swing through the push bars. I was in!

Mike Cunningham, the team leader, introduced me to the two-man Bob. I was to be brakeman.

John Blockey, my driver, showed me the bend called "Bridge". "We'll come out of this at 80 mph," he told me.

I practised getting "locked in" behind John on a stationary Bob.

This was it! One - two - three - and we were off for the ride of a lifetime!

Seconds after this picture was taken we hit a hole in the ice.

I completed the course on my backside and was picked up by Mike and John Craig.

I had bruises as proof for six weeks afterwards, as 8 million viewers will testify.

The exhilaration was beyond description. I was aware of a great white wall coming towards me, my breath was pushed back down my throat, and my stomach left half up the mountain as we came out of "Sunny" like an express train.

"Horseshoe" next. For a flash I remembered standing 8 metres below our present position as John beautifully judged the bend to send us hurtling out at a promised 80 mph. My chin hit my chest as the force of gravity made my head feel like lead — but we were all right . . .

It was just after "Bridge" that I met my Waterloo. There was one small hole in the ice wall, and by a million to one chance, we hit it. The next thing I knew, I was upside down with the Bob on top of me, still travelling at over 80 mph. I fought like fury to get out. I was trapped for what seemed like hours, but I was afterwards told it was about eight seconds. The next thing I knew was a sensation of flying, followed by the biggest battering I ever had in my life. Then I was

totally aware of roaring down the bob run in the approved position — the only problem was, I had no sledge! I completed the course on my backside, and I had bruises to prove it for about six weeks afterwards.

When I eventually came to a standstill, they told me I got up and started walking back up the course — but I don't remember much at all — except for a terrific pain in the bottom. Mike and the boys all came and rallied round, and helped me back to where we'd left the car. They told me that John, miraculously, had been able to right the sledge and that he was okay. I remember breathing in the lovely, cold, clear air, and looking at the snow on the mountainside and thinking how good it was to be alive.

FOOTNOTE:

It is typical of John Noakes that the first thing he did when they picked him up out of the snow was to ask if John, the driver, was all right — and the next thing he did was to make a joke.

Editors.

DIGGING FOR DINNER

A sack full of beans, non-stop lettuces from May to January, pound after pound of turnips and carrots, bunches of flowers all through the summer, and a giant-sized pumpkin plant with miniature fruit!

That was just part of the harvest from our first efforts at gardening — and when you consider that our plot measures only 3½ by 3½ metres, and that every single plant was grown from packets of seed that cost only a few pence a piece, we reckon that all the digging, watering and weeding, was really worthwhile. Mind you, we couldn't have done it without top gardener Percy Thrower to start us off and show us exactly what to do.

We dug up some grass on a piece of ground at the back of our canteen at the Television Centre on 21 March 1974. From then on, there was no stopping us. Here's our diary of a year's work on the Blue Peter garden.

MARCH:

The first big dig. It didn't take long to prepare the ground. Percy showed us what to plant. There were peas, parsley, lettuce and radishes. "How do we do it?" we asked. "Follow the directions on the seed packets," said Percy, "and you won't go far wrong." John spilled a few radishes, but on the whole we did quite a neat job. Planted some mustard and cress on trays of wet felt too, and brought them indoors.

APRIL:

Mustard and cress grown and eaten long since! Vegetable seeds going well, too. Everything's grown up about 4 cms — including the radish seeds John spilled! Put some lettuce in and planted mixed flower seeds. Are now hoping for a good show in the summer. Percy showed us how to take cuttings from a geranium. We've put some in pots on the wall.

MAY:

Radishes ready for eating and very good, too. First lot of lettuces ready to eat, so we've sent them to the Old People's Centre at Deptford. Transplanted the new lettuce seeds to give them space and light. Planted runner beans and sweet peas.

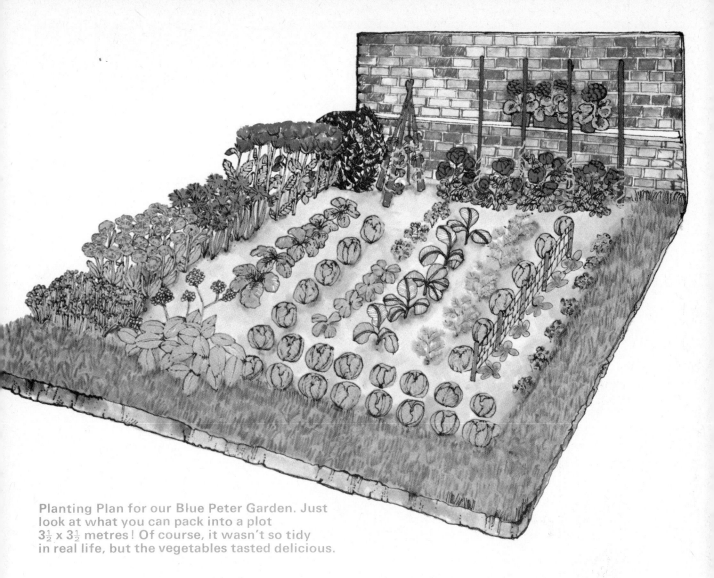

Planting Plan for our Blue Peter Garden. Just look at what you can pack into a plot 3½ x 3½ metres! Of course, it wasn't so tidy in real life, but the vegetables tasted delicious.

JUNE:

Sweet peas very straggly. "They need support," said Percy, so we built cane "wig-wams" for them to grow up. Runner beans racing up the wall. Mr Charlie Roberts, champion pumpkin grower, gave us two seeds. "Where shall we plant them?" said Pete. "A long way from everything else!" said Percy. "Those two seeds could swamp every other plant." Pete put them in by the nesting box—no eggs again—but better luck with pumpkins, maybe!

JULY:

The radishes have "bolted"! They've gone long and straggly with white flowers on top and soggy roots below. We should have eaten them, but it's too late now! The dreaded black fly is all over everything! "Finish them off with Derris powder," said Percy, and showed us how to spray. Went to Thailand on our Expedition and hoped for the best.

SEPTEMBER:

Came back from Thailand to huge quantities of beans (our best crop), good turnips and beetroots, some rather scraggy lettuce that the birds had eaten while we were away, and a gigantic pumpkin plant with 3-metre tendrils

and the world's smallest pumpkins!
Mr Roberts' own pumpkin weighed 34 kilos., so it seems we just don't have the knack! We sent our best vegetables to the Old People's Centre and they really were a splendid basket full. Planted daffodils, crocuses and tulips ready for the spring.

OCTOBER:

"What shall we do with the pumpkin plant?" said Pete. "It'll make splendid compost!" said Percy. So planting those seeds wasn't a waste of time, and from the tiny fruit, Lesley made a miniature pumpkin lantern for Hallowe'en. Beans still going strong.

NOVEMBER:

Tidied up the plot and dug it over. Nothing to do now till next spring.

JANUARY:

Some lettuce still growing! It's a bit odd-looking but we've dug it up and it'll be just right for a winter salad.

FEBRUARY:

Bulbs coming up. "Let's try potatoes as well this year," said Percy, so we've turned the soil over and now we're ready to start all over again.

Never forget a face

Mary Evans at the Slimbridge Wild Fowl Trust can tell you the name of every Bewick Swan on the lake. When I first arrived, I didn't know the difference between a Mute and a Bewick Swan, but after half a day with Mary, even I was able to recognise a couple of Bewicks.

Every October, the Bewick swans fly south into the comparatively mild British climate to escape the rigours of a Russian winter. Bewicks, which are named after a famous ornithologist, are smaller and a good deal noisier than the mute swans that live all the year round in Britain.

I met Mary, a slight, attractive, dark-haired Scottish girl, in the Swan Observatory at Slimbridge. She was looking through a pair of binoculars at the great mass of birds on the lake. Slimbridge, near Gloucester, is the greatest centre for wild fowl in Britain. There's a huge permanent collection of birds that stay there all the year round, but in winter, they're joined by thousands of migrants.

"I'm just drawing a new swan that arrived today," said Mary, looking up from her sketch pad. She explained that every swan had different individual markings on its bill, so you can clearly tell one from the

Every time a new bird arrives, Mary draws its head and gives it a name.

She can tell you the name of every single Bewick swan on the lake.

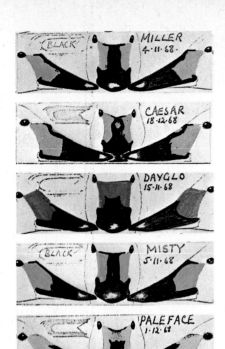

Every Bewick swan has unique markings. To Mary they're as different as humans.

This solitary swan called Leopard, was wounded, and his mate, Puma, killed when

they flew off to some flooded meadows – although shooting swans is against the law.

other.

"Like a human's finger print?" I asked.

"No, more like a face," she replied.

Mary showed me an enormous chart full of beautifully drawn heads of swans.

"You see, Miller is black from the tip of his beak to the feathering, whereas Caesar has a yellow patch in the middle, and with May, the black stops half-way. And colouring is sometimes different, too. Take DayGlo, for instance, he's quite orange, but Misty here has a bright yellow bill, and Paleface is yellower still."

There were four swans on the far side of the lake stretching their necks and making the most ferocious honking noises.

"They're birds from the permanent collection," explained Mary, "and they don't like those two wild swans occupying their territory."

Swans are monogamous – they have one mate and they stay together all their lives until one of them dies. That's why you always see them in pairs; so I was rather surprised to see one solitary bird in the middle of the crowded lake.

"That's Leopard," said Mary. "He came here first about six years ago with his mate, Puma, but they didn't return the following year. In fact, we didn't see either of them again until this winter."

"They both came back together?" I asked.

"Yes, they did. But when the surrounding fields got flooded in the recent heavy rains, they flew off and they stayed away for about three weeks. Then one day, Leopard returned alone – looking very bedraggled, and with a nasty limp. We managed to catch him and got him X-rayed. It was then that we found that he was full of shot."

"Do you think Puma must have been killed?" I asked.

"I'm afraid so – although shooting swans is strictly against the law."

Mary is a professional ornithologist, and the death of one of the birds on the lake is something she has to get used to.

But I could see that if, like Mary, I could name every swan on the lake by looking at its face, I'd feel very sad when one of those faces disappeared for ever.

All the birds on the swan lake at Slimbridge are fed every morning at 8 o'clock.

There are six swans in the permanent collection, but every autumn they are joined by about 500 winter visitors.

Harvington looks very ordinary from the outside. It's a picturesque, moated Elizabethan house with brick walls and gabled roofs all huddled together at different levels. Inside, too, there seem to be few surprises as you pass through the panelled dining-room with its great open fireplace and climb the stairs to the bedroom of Lady Yate who was lady of the house 300 years ago.

In one corner there is a door which leads to a closet where there is a kind of primitive lavatory directly over the moat – draughty, but effective! Here too there is a wooden floor, and if you bang on it, it sounds solid.

HOUSE OF SECRETS

A hinged panel in the Library revealed a hiding place just big enough for a man to squeeze through.

And once inside, the space was enough to hide him whilst the house was searched.

But this floor holds a secret – the first of the secrets of Harvington Hall. If you know how, you can lift up a trap-door. It is very heavy because it is three layers of wood thick, which is why it doesn't sound hollow.

Below the trap-door is a secret room. I peered in with my torch and could see it measured about $1\frac{1}{2}$ metres by 1 metre, and was 2 metres high. A man could stay concealed in the space so that no one would know he was there. But why should he want to? Who would want to hide in such a dark and uncomfortable place? What had he to fear?

I found the answer lay more than four hundred years back. At that time, England was torn by cruel religious divisions. Protestants and Catholics were enemies, each side wanting everyone to accept their beliefs.

Queen Elizabeth I was on the throne. She was a Protestant, and she declared that she was sovereign of the Church of England, too. Everyone was ordered to attend Church of England services.

Catholics who would not had to pay heavy fines. If they went to services of the Catholic style, they could be arrested and carried off to prison.

The men in most danger were the priests who celebrated the service. They were arrested and tried, and savagely put to death as traitors to their Queen and Country. Most Catholics were not traitors at all, but they were determined to carry on with their religion, whatever price they had to pay.

In tiny groups, men landed secretly in England from the continent. They were Englishmen who had been trained as priests abroad, and had come home at desperate risk to themselves. Disguised and secretly, they went to Catholic homes up and down the country, to say Mass to the families who lived there. They were in constant danger, and the householder, too, was in peril while the priest was under his roof.

Nicholas Owen, a Catholic, was a small, quiet man, who limped because of a fall from a horse. He was not a priest – he was a builder and carpenter. He would go to a house to make some building alterations that the owner had ordered. Then, during the night, he would carry out his real work. Somewhere, in the walls, under the floor, behind the chimney, he would build a secret hiding place – a priest's hole where a hunted priest might lie hidden until danger was past. Only the owner of the house was told exactly where it was.

Nicholas Owen was a very small man – he was nicknamed Little John – and some of his hiding places must have been a tight fit for a tall priest. But Little John was a master craftsman.

"Many priests," Catholics declared gratefully, "have been saved by secret places of his making."

The danger to Catholic priests continued. Spies were everywhere. Men called pursuivants tracked them down, promised a reward of £50 for every priest they caught. They took builders and carpenters with them who probed and measured everywhere, almost pulling a suspected house to pieces. Only after days of fruitless search would they give up!

A simple table would serve as an altar when the faithful came together.

A shout from the look-out and the "Church things" would be hidden away.

At last Nicholas Owen himself was captured and there was no escape. He was tortured to make him say where he had built his hiding places, but he knew that this would mean betraying everyone who had trusted him. He died very bravely, refusing to say a word.

Because Nicholas Owen kept quiet, there is still a mystery about his hiding places. Hundreds of priests' holes have been found in houses all over the country, but we cannot be sure who built them to this day.

No one is certain if the secret places in Harvington Hall were made by Nicholas Owen, or by another skilled man who came after him. One thing is certain – for many years after Little John's death, Harvington Hall was the stronghold of a Catholic family who would gather with a handful of their Catholic neighbours in a room at the top of the house, which they had made into a chapel. A tiny altar, that could be moved away, was set up and before it, the priest – the man with the price on his head – would begin the forbidden service of the Mass.

Next door to the chapel is a big room, still known as Lady Yate's nursery. One trusted person, perhaps the nurse, would stay there throughout the service. The wall looks solid, but it is really only a thin partition so that she could follow the priest's words. And all the time, she looked out of the window, over the moat, across the quiet countryside.

Then, suddenly, she might see horses – a flash of metal – officers from the town, suspecting something. They had to cross the bridge, knock and wait while the door was opened. The worshippers could reckon on two or three minutes. The nurse knocked hard on the wall. The Mass ended. In the chapel, swiftly, calmly, the "church things" as they called them were bundled together – chalice, crucifix, the priest's vestments, the altar itself. The owner of the house trod hard on a particular notch in the skirting board. It released a catch, so that a floor-board could be lifted, and the church things stowed away. The congregation scattered, and the priest hid – sometimes with only seconds to spare.

He dodged on the landing where each step of the oak staircase looks solid, but he knew how to move the short flight of steps and get into the cavity behind, just large enough for him to crouch down, while the steps were pushed to, behind him. In the cavity, he would feel for the hinges and bolts of another door, and get into a tiny room behind – it measured about two metres square and was $1\frac{1}{2}$ metres high. When this hide was discovered, after many years, a rush mattress was found lying on the floor to give a scrap of comfort to the fugitive as he huddled listening to the banging and the muffled knocks, and the shouts of the searchers, for hours or perhaps days, until it was safe for him to clamber out into the daylight again.

The secret nooks and crannies are countless. Even the kitchen provided shelter of a kind. Inside the huge hearth by the side of the great chimney is a shaft which held the ropes and weights for turning the spit on which the huge joints of meat were roasted. The shaft leads directly to the hiding place in the closet above, under the floor of Lady Yate's lavatory. A very active man could wriggle out of that hole, down the spitshaft, holding the rope, and with luck, get out and pass himself off as one of the kitchen servants. Altogether, seven hiding places have been discovered at Harvington

The priest would disappear into any of a dozen hiding places.

Hall. They must have been good hides, because in spite of all the suspicions of neighbours, the eagerness of the searchers, the bribes and rewards, no one was ever arrested there; the secret places were never discovered by an enemy. The skill of the builder, and the steadfastness of the Catholic believers, got them through the bad years.

Gradually, the house was lived in less and less.

For many years, it lay empty, and time stood still at Harvington Hall. The secret places were forgotten.

Only slowly has the story been pieced together, and all the hiding places been rediscovered.

I made my way from Harvington Hall, and turned to look back from the garden. My eyes wandered over its twisted shape.

Then, I couldn't help wondering. Did all those chimneys lead straight to fireplaces? Has every space under the sloping roofs been accounted for? Or are there more gaps, under the floors and between walls, that time has not yet revealed?

Is it possible that Harvington Hall, that House of Secrets, keeps some secrets still?

MYSTERY PICTURE

Colour the spaces as indicated by the numbers and the mystery picture will appear

1 Red
2 Yellow
3 Black
4 Green
5 Dark Blue
6 Pink
7 Brown
8 Light Blue
9 Grey

PUZZLE PICTURES
1 We gave the boys of Bletchley Boys' Brigade some good practice before the start of their **Spud Bashing** fund-raising scheme.
2 Hundreds of badges decorate William Gough's lorry.
3 **An electric exercise** horse, now owned privately, **Ironsides** used to belong to the liner Queen Mary.
4 In our **Waiters' Obstacle Race,** John competed against Gilberto from Italy, Erdogan from Turkey, Pepe from Spain and Gunay from Cyprus.
5 Wearing full Everest climbing gear and dangling from the studio roof, Peter was given some tips by Dave Clarke, a member of **Chris Bonington's British Everest Expedition, 1975.**
6 **Percy Thrower** plus twin? No, just Percy plus his shirt-sleeved double, made in wax for Madame Tussaud's Exhibition.
7 The underground well at **Chenies Manor** in Buckinghamshire explored by John and members of the **Watford Underwater Club.**
8 This giant telephone, and the books and cotton reel, were made for a trick sequence in **Charlie Drake's** film, *Professor Popper's Pills.*
9 **Massed piano playing** by the girls of the John Howard School in London's East End. With 32 hands playing 8 concert grand pianos, plus 8 percussion instruments, Stravinsky's "Firebird" sounded most impressive.

SPECIAL ASSIGNMENT
1 Tiger Balm Gardens.
2 Children's Paint-In.
3 The Yaumati Typhoon Shelter.
4 Queen Victoria's bed.
5 Valerie with Lord Mountbatten, K.G., O.M., D.S.O., Lord Lieutenant and Governor of the Isle of Wight.
6 Queen Victoria's Bathing Machine.
7 & 9 Mad Sunday at the TT Races, Isle of Man.
8 A 500 cc race – Isle of Man.
10 In Bonnie Prince Charlie's footsteps.
11 With Dame Flora MacLeod, 97-year old 28th Chieftain of the Clan MacLeod.
12 The ruins of Monkstad House where Bonnie Prince Charlie hid.
13 Outside St Publius' Church in Valletta.
14 In the Hypogeum.
15 Outside the Citadel Church, Gozo.

THE CASE OF THE MALTESE CROSS
1 The M1 Motorway starts at London and goes north, so Mr Fennelon could not have driven on it from Dover to London.
2 Minestrone is an Italian soup, and not a Mediterranean wind!
3 Malta is in the Mediterranean, and not in the Black Sea.
4 Malta is a true island, and is not connected to any mainland. It has no causeway to Sicily.
5 Malta G.C. is the only country to have been awarded a medal in the Second World War – but it was the George Cross (G.C.) and not the Victoria Cross (V.C.)
6 Professor Johnston told his audience that the Cross was to be displayed at an Exhibition at the Royal Academy, not the National Gallery as the impostor Fennelon had stated.

USEFUL INFORMATION
Blue Peter Books
Blue Peter Special Assignment London, Amsterdam & Edinburgh.
Blue Peter Special Assignment Rome, Paris & Vienna.
Blue Peter Special Assignment Venice & Brussels.
Blue Peter Special Assignment Madrid, Dublin & York.
Blue Peter Special Assignment Hong Kong & Malta.
Blue Peter Special Assignment Isle of Sky, Isle of Man & Isle of Wight.
Blue Peter Book of Limericks.
Paddington's Blue Peter Story Book.
Blue Peter Book of Odd Odes. (to be published late 1975).

Blue Peter Inshore Life Boats
Blue Peter I –
Littlehampton (a 21-foot Atlantic boat) .
Secretary: Peter Cheney
Tel: Littlehampton 3922
Blue Peter II –
Beaumaris (a 16-foot Inshore Rescue boat shortly to be replaced by a 21-foot Atlantic boat).
Secretary: Lieutenant Colonel V. J. C. Cooper.
Tel: Menai Bridge 713227
Blue Peter III –
North Berwick (a 16-foot Inshore Rescue boat).
Secretary: F. Cessford, O.B.E.
Tel: North Berwick 3218
Blue Peter IV –
St Agnes (a 16-foot Inshore Rescue boat).
Secretary: E. G. Simmons.
Tel: St Agnes 2307

Guide Dogs for the Blind Association
113 Uxbridge Road, London W.5.
Puppy Walking Manager:
Tollgate House, Banbury Road, Bishops Tachbrook, Leamington Spa, Warks.
Regional Centres:
Bolton, Exeter, Forfar, Leamington Spa, Wokingham (open 1976).

Slimbridge Wildfowl Trust, Slimbridge, Nr Gloucester.

Harvington Hall
Chaddesley Corbett, Nr Kidderminster, Worcs.
Tel: 056-283 267.

Thailand Tourist Organisation
Chichester House, 278 High Holborn, London W.C.1.

White Helmets
Catterick Camp, Yorkshire.

Cockney Museum
9/10 Floral Street, Old Covent Garden, W.C.2.

ACKNOWLEDGEMENTS
The House of Secrets was written by Dorothy Smith; *The Runaways* was illustrated by Robert Broomfield; *Bleep & Booster* and the *Mystery Picture* by "Tim"; *The Case of the Maltese Cross* was illustrated by Bernard Blatch; The R 101 by Geoffrey Wheeler.
Photographs in this book were taken by:
Joan Williams, Charles Walls, Barry Boxall, John Jefford, John Adcock, Rosemary Gill, Crispan Woodgate, Victor Camilleri, Calum Neish, Ray Cranbourne, Mary Evans and Peter Dobson, with the exception of Corpus Christi College (p. 35) by Camera Press; Pearly Christening (p. 6) and R101 wreck (p. 50/51) by Radio Times Hulton Picture Library; the Pearly dog (p. 6) is reproduced by permission of Adam Joseph's Cockney Museum; the Pearly Princess (p. 6) is reproduced from *Pearly Kings and Queens in Britain* by Peter Brooks, Barry Rose Publishers, Little London, Chichester. Inset picture of Elizabeth Barrett Browning (p. 44) from the National Portrait Gallery.
BIDDY BAXTER, EDWARD BARNES AND ROSEMARY GILL WOULD LIKE TO ACKNOWLEDGE THE HELP OF GILLIAN FARNSWORTH AND MARGARET PARNELL.

Designed by
Eileen Strange & John Strange

BLUE PETER Competition

Here's your chance to meet the Blue Peter Team at the
BBC TV Centre.
The first prize will be an invitation to a
Blue Peter Party
which includes a trip round the studios, a chance to watch
the Blue Peter rehearsals and have tea with the Blue Peter
team – not forgetting the animals! There will be lots of
competition badges for the runners-up, too.

BLUE PETER PARTY

Here are nine yellow labradors. Three of them are Blue Peter
Guide Dog puppies – Honey, Cindy and Buttons. Can you spot
which ones they are? When you've decided, fill in the numbers
beside their names on the entry form.

- ✂

Cut out your entry and send it to:
Blue Peter Competition, BBC TV Centre, London W12.

Honey is Number.......

Cindy is Number........

Buttons is Number....

Name_____ Age_____

Address_____

_____

First-prize winners and runners-up will be notified by letter.
The closing date for entries is 10 January 1976.

START→

BLUE PETER SPEED MAZE

This isn't as complicated as Greg Bright's maze on page 48, but the idea is

WAY OUT?

WAY OUT ↑?